The Science of Getting Rich
by Wallace Wattles

$

Updated for the 21st Century
by Dr. Jane Ma'ati Smith C.Hyp. Msc.D.

"The Universe desires you to have everything you want to
have. Nature is friendly to you plans. Everything is naturally
for you."

"Make up your mind this is true. You need not hesitate
about asking largely."

~Wallace Wattles

ISBN# 1438234937   EAN-13# 9781438234939

TABLE OF CONTENTS

This book is primarily the original version by Wallace Wattles, with updated language and additional information by Dr. Jane Ma'ati Smith, C.Hyp. Msc.D.

To truly experience the power of this approach to prosperity, make sure you also have the self hypnosis and subliminal binaural beat CD, "The Science of Getting Rich" by Dr. Jane Ma'ati Smith C.Hyp. Msc.D. It is available on Amazon.com or on Dr. Smith's website at www.subliminalselfhypnosis.com

I would like to acknowledge all the masters of manifestation, both classic and modern. T. Harv Eker for giving us the Secrets of the Millionaire Mind, Napoleoon Hill for the ability to Think and Grow Rich, Donald Trump for all his brassy and bold individuality, Robert T. Kiyosaki for being our adopted Rich Dad, Rhonda Byrne for giving us The Secret, as well as Hale Dwoskin, Mike Dooley, Bill Harris, Fred Alan Wolf, Dennis Waitley, Marci Shimoff, John F. DeMartini Marie Diamond, Michael Beckwith, Lee Brower, Morris Goodman, Bob Proctor, John Assaraf, James Ray, Joe Vitale and Esther Hicks Abraham for sharing their Secrets too.

I would also like to thank Nightingale Conant for all their very good books and audio programs. I would like to thank the amazing Catherine Ponder, and Edwene Gaines for the The Four Spiritual Laws of Prosperity: A Simple Guide to Unlimited Abundance. David Wann for his brand of Simple Prosperity and Finding Real Wealth in a Sustainable Lifestyle, Charles Fillmore, Suze Orman for the 9 steps to Financial Freedom, and Dave Ramsey for giving us a total money makeover. Stuart E. Lucas for Wealth: Grow It, Protect It, Spend It, and Share It. James Arthur Ray for Harmonic Wealth. Jeffrey D. Sachs for his common sense Common Wealth: Economics for a Crowded Planet, and Pat Dorsey for The Little Book That Builds Wealth. Keith Cameron Smith, David Bach, and Douglas R. Andrew, Emron Andrew, and Aaron Andrew.

Thomas J. Stanley and William D. Danko for being The Millionaire Next Door, Thomas J. Stanley for his view of The Millionaire Mind, Mark Victor Hansen and Robert G. Allen for The One Minute Millionaire, Conor O'Clery for introducing us to the billionaire who wasn't, Chuck Feeney. Scot Anderson for Think Like a Billionaire, Become a Billionaire. John D. MacArthur for being our favorite Eccentric Billionaire.

Robert Frank for his guided tour of "Richistan". David Bach for showing sart women how to finish rich. Rosemary Wells for teaching kids with Bunny Money. Jim Cramer for giving us Sane Investing in an Insane World.

And of course, I would like to thank you, the reader, for taking the positive steps necessary to enrich not only your life, but the lives of everyone around you, with the practices set forth in this book!

Preface

This book is primarily a practical guide, not a philosophical treatise on theories, though theory you will also get. It is for those who have found neither the time, the means, nor the opportunity to go deeply into the study of metaphysics, but who want results, and are willing to take the conclusions of quantum physics as a basis for action, without going into all the processes by which these theories were reached.

I hope you will take the fundamental statements in this book on faith, just as you would take statements concerning a law of physics by Einstein or Hawking on faith, and that you will prove the truth of the fundamental principles in this book by acting without fear or hesitation. Everyone who does this, sincerely and unceasingly, will certainly get rich; failure is ultimately impossible, for those who truly believe.

The monistic theory of the Universe is the theory that One is All, and that All is One. That one "substance" or energy (which some call God) manifests itself as the seemingly many different elements of the material world. Imagine a tapestry, woven with many different colors and textures, forming different patterns and pictures, yet it is all the same cloth. This metaphysical theory is ancient, and has been winning its way into the thought of the modern Western world for many years. The theory that one "substance" or energy permeating, penetrating and manifesting itself as All That Is has recently manifested itself in the modern theories of Quantum Physics. (For a great, fun "beginner's guide" to Quantum Physics, rent or buy the award winning film What the Bleep!? Starring Marlee Matlin.)

The plan of action which follows grew from the study of philosophy, metaphysics, and of various religions; it has been time tested, and passes the supreme test of practical experiment; it works!

CHAPTER 1- Your Right To Be Rich

Whatever might be said in praise of poverty, the fact remains that it's not possible to live a really complete or successful life unless you have money. No one can rise to their greatest potential personal development unless they have plenty of money; if you want to develop your talent, your soul, or just live the "good life", you will need time and things, and you cannot have things or time unless you have money.

A person develops in mind, soul, and body by making use of time and things, and society is so organized that you must have money in order to get things, and to make time; therefore, the basis of all advancement must ultimately be the quantum science of getting rich.

The object of all life is to develop; and everything that lives has an inalienable right to all the development it is capable of.

Your right to life means your right to have the free and unrestricted use of all the things which may be necessary to develop your full mental, spiritual, and physical development; or, in other words, your right to be rich.

In this book, I won't speak of riches in a figurative way; to be really rich does not mean to be satisfied or contented with just a little. No one ought to be satisfied with a little if they are capable of more. The purpose of Nature is the advancement and development of life; and everyone should have all that can contribute to the energy, elegance, beauty, and richness of life.

The person who owns what they want, for living all the life they are capable of, is rich. Life has advanced so far, and become so complex, that even the most ordinary man or woman requires a great amount of money in order to live in a manner that even approaches completeness. Everyone naturally wants to become all they are capable of becoming; this desire to realize innate possibilities is inherent to your human nature; we can't help wanting to be all that we can be. Success in life is becoming what you want to be; you can become what you want to be only by making use of resources, and you can have the free use of resources only if you have enough money to buy them. To understand the science behind getting rich is therefore the most essential of all knowledge.

There is nothing wrong in wanting to get rich. The desire for riches is really the desire for a richer, fuller, and more abundant life; and that desire is praise worthy. The person who does not want to live more abundantly is not normal; and consequently, the person who does not want to have money to buy all he wants is not normal. Harsh, but true.

There are three aspect of ourselves for which we live; we live for the body, we live for the mind, we live for the soul. No one of these is better than the other; all are important, and none of the three, body, mind, or soul, can live fully if the other two is cut short of life and expression. It is not right or noble to live only for the soul and deny the mind or body; and it is wrong to live for the intellect and deny body and soul.

We have all seen the awful consequences of living for the body and denying both the mind and soul; and we see that *real* life means the complete expression of all that you can give through body, mind, and soul. Whatever you can say, no one can be really happy or satisfied unless their body is fully functioning, and the same is true of the mind and soul. Wherever there is unexpressed possibility, or function not performed, there is an unsatisfied desire. Desire is possibility seeking expression, or function seeking performance.

You cannot live fully in body without good food, comfortable clothing, and adequate shelter; and without freedom from excessive work! Rest and recreation are also necessary to your physical life.

You cannot live fully in mind without books and the time to read them, without the opportunity for travel, or without intellectual companionship.

To live fully in mind you must have intellectual pursuits, and surround yourself with all the objects of art and beauty you are capable of using and appreciating.

To live fully in soul, you must have love; and love is denied full expression by poverty. A person's highest happiness is found in benefiting those they love; love finds its most natural and spontaneous expression in giving. The person who has nothing to give can't fill their place as a husband or father, wife or mother, or as a contributing citizen in society. It is in the use of material things that a person finds full life to nourish the body, develop the mind, and unfold the soul. It is important to be rich.

It is perfectly alright that you wish to be rich; if you are a normal person, you can't help it! It is perfectly alright that you give your attention to getting rich, for it is the most necessary of all studies. If you neglect this study, you are derelict in your duty to yourself, to God and to humanity; for you can render to God and humanity no greater service than to make the most of yourself.

CHAPTER 2- The Quantum Science of Getting Rich

There is a quantum science to getting rich, and it's an exact science, like algebra or math. There are certain laws, which govern the process of acquiring wealth; once these laws are learned and obeyed by anyone, they will get rich with a mathematical certainty.

The ownership of money and property comes as a result of doing things in a certain way; those who do things in this certain way, whether on purpose or accidentally, get rich; those who do not do things in this certain way, no matter how hard they work, or how able they are, remain poor.

It is a natural law, that like cause always produce like results; therefore, anyone who learns to do things in this certain way will invariably get rich.

That the above statement is true is shown by the following facts:

Getting rich is not a matter of environment- if it were, all the people in certain neighborhoods would become wealthy; the people of one city would all be rich, while those of other towns would all be poor; or the inhabitants of one state would roll in wealth, while those of an adjoining state would be in poverty.

But everywhere we see rich and poor living side by side, in the same environments, and often doing the same jobs. When two people are in the same locality, and in the same business, and one gets rich while the other remains poor, it shows that getting rich is not primarily a matter of environment. Some environments might be more favorable than others, but when two people in the same business are in the same neighborhood, and one gets rich while the other fails, it indicates that getting rich is the result of doing things in a certain way.

And, the ability to do things in a certain way is not due solely to talent, for many people who have greater talent remain poor, while others who have very little talent get rich.

Studying the people who got rich, we find that they are an average lot in most respects, having no greater talent and ability than most people. Evidently, they don't get rich because they possess talents and abilities that others do not, but because they happen to do things in different way.

Getting rich is not the result of saving, or "thrift"; many thrifty people are poor, while free spenders often get rich.

Nor is getting rich due to doing things which others fail to do; two people in the same business often do almost exactly the same things, and one gets rich while the other remains poor, or worse, becomes bankrupt.

From this, we must come to the conclusion that getting rich is the result of doing things in a certain way.

If getting rich is the result of doing things in a certain way, and if like cause always produce a like result, then anyone who can do things in that way can be rich.

The question is, whether this certain way of doing things is so difficult that only a few may follow it. Some degree of ability to think and understand is, of course, essential; but as far as natural ability is concerned, anyone who has sense enough to read and understand these words can certainly get rich. If you can make up your mind to truly do so, all you will have to do is change the way you think and act, and this will be as difficult as you allow it to be, or as easy as you allow it to be, it all depends on how easy you want to make it. *(And I will help you make it as easy as possible to literally "change your mind" with the binaural beat self hypnosis program. See Appendix A for more details.)*

We have seen that it's not a matter of environment. Location counts for something; getting rich involves the necessity of dealing with people, and of being where there are people to deal with; and if these people are inclined to deal in the way you want to deal, so much the better. But that is about as far as environment goes.

If anybody else in your town can get rich, so can you; and if anybody else in your state can get rich, so can you.

Again, it is not a matter of choosing some particular business or profession. People get rich in every business, and in every profession; while their next door neighbors in the same vocation remain poor.

It's true you will do best in a business you like, and if you have certain talents which are well developed, you will do best in a business which calls for those talents.

Also, you will do best in a business which is suited to your locality; a surfboard shop will do better in Hawaii or California than in Ohio! But aside from some general limits, getting rich is not dependent on your engaging in some particular business, but upon your learning to do things in a certain way. If you are now in business, and anybody else in your locality is getting rich in the same business, while you are not getting rich, it is because you are not doing things in the same way the other person is doing them.

No one is prevented from getting rich by a lack of capital. True, as you gain capital, the increase becomes more easy and rapid; but someone who has capital is already rich! No matter how poor you may be, if you begin to do things in the certain way, you will begin to get rich; and you will begin to have capital. The getting of capital is a part of the process of getting rich; it is a part of the result which invariably follows the doing of things in a certain way. You may be the poorest person on the continent, deep in debt; you may have no friends, no influence, no resources; but if you begin to do things in this way, you *must* begin to get rich, for like causes must produce like results. If you have no capital, you can get capital; if you are in the wrong business, you can get into the right business; if you are in the wrong location, you can go to the right location; and you can do so *by beginning in your present business and in your present location* to do things in the certain way which causes success!

CHAPTER 3- Is Opportunity Monopolized?

No one is kept poor because opportunity has been taken away from them; because other people have monopolized the wealth, and put a fence around it. You may be cut off from certain businesses, but there are other channels open to you. It would probably be hard for you to gain control of an airline or oil corporation; those fields are pretty well monopolized! But look around you- what service can you provide? Where do your natural talents and abilities lean? I am sure you will find something in which to succeed!

It is quite true that if you are working in a big corporation, you have very little chance of becoming the CEO; but it is also true that if you commence to act in a certain way, you can soon leave the corporate world, and do you own thing!

At different times, the tide of opportunity sets in different directions, according to the needs of the whole, and the particular stage of social evolution which we find ourselves in. There is abundance of opportunity for the person who will go with the tide, instead of trying to swim against it- look around, see what the trends are, and how you can fill a need with your particular talents, tastes and inclinations.

So the corporate workers and wage slaves, either as individuals or as a class, are not deprived of opportunity. The workers are not being "kept down" by their masters; they are not being "ground down" by the CEO's and corporate conglomerates. As a class, they are where they are because they do not do things in a certain way. If the workers of America chose to do so, they could follow the example of their forefathers, and strike out on their own! The working class may become the master class when they begin to do things in a certain way; the law of wealth is the same for them as it is for others. The individual worker is not held down by their class; you can follow the tide of opportunity to riches.

No one is kept in poverty by a short supply of wealth; there is more than enough for all. A nice home could be built for every family on earth, and with wise and ecological cultivation, this world could produce enough food enough to feed everyone as well. The visible supply is practically inexhaustible; and the invisible supply really IS inexhaustible.

Everything you see on earth is made from one original substance, out of which all things proceed.

New Forms are constantly being made, and older ones are dissolving; but all are shapes assumed by One Thing.

There is no limit to the supply of Formless Stuff, Original Substance, God, Goddess, Energy, or whatever you choose to call It. The Universe is made out of it; but it was not all used up in making the Universe! The spaces in, through, and between the forms of the visible world are permeated and filled with this Original Substance; with the Formless Stuff; with Energy, the raw material of all things. Ten thousand times as much as has been made, and might still be made, and even then we would not have exhausted the supply of Universal Energy, the raw material!

No one is poor because nature is poor, or because there is not enough to go around. Nature can be an inexhaustible storehouse of riches; the supply will never run short. Original Substance is alive with creative energy, and is constantly producing more forms. When the supply of building material is exhausted, more will be produced; when the soil is exhausted, it will be renewed, or more soil will be made somewhere else. When all the gold and silver has been dug from the ground, if Mankind is still in such a stage of social development that they need gold and silver, more will produced from the Formless. The Formless Stuff responds to the needs of Mankind; it will not let it be without any good thing.

This is true of Mankind collectively; people as a whole are always abundantly rich, and if individuals are poor, it is because they do not follow the certain way of doing things, which makes the individual person rich.

The Formless Stuff is intelligent; it is stuff which *thinks*. It is alive, and is always impelled toward more *life*.

It is the natural and inherent impulse of life to seek to live more; it is the nature of intelligence to enlarge itself, and of consciousness to seek to extend its boundaries and find fuller expression. The Universe of forms has been made by Formless Living Substance, throwing itself into form, in order to express itself more fully.

The Universe is a great Living Presence, always moving inherently toward more life and fuller functioning.

Nature is formed for the advancement of life; its impelling motive is the increase of life. For this reason, everything which can possibly add to and nurture life is bountifully provided; there can be no lack, unless "God" is to contradict itself and nullify its own work.

You are not kept poor by a lack in the supply of riches; it is a fact which I shall demonstrate a little farther on, that even the resources of the Formless Supply are at the command of the person that acts and thinks in a certain way.

CHAPTER 4- The First Principle of Getting Rich

Thought is the only power which can produce tangible riches from the Formless Substance. The stuff from which all things are made is a substance which thinks, and a thought of form in this substance produces the form.

Original Substance moves according to its thoughts; every form and process you see in nature is the visible expression of a thought in Original Substance (often referred to as "God". So everything you see can be thought of as a thought of "God"). As the Formless Stuff thinks of a form, it takes that form; as it thinks of a motion, it makes that motion. That is the way all things were created. We live in a thought world, which

14

is part of a thought Universe. The thought of a moving Universe, extended throughout Formless Substance, and the Thinking Stuff moving according to that thought, took the form of systems of planets, and maintains that form. Thinking Substance takes the form of its thought, and moves according to the thought. Holding the idea of a circling system of suns and worlds, it takes the form of these bodies, and moves them as it thinks. Thinking the form of a slow-growing oak tree, it moves accordingly, and produces the tree, though centuries may be required to do the work. In creating, the Formless seems to move according to the lines of motion it has already established; the thought of an oak tree does not cause the instant formation of a full-grown tree, but it does start in motion the forces which will produce the tree, along established lines of growth.

Every thought of form, held in Thinking Substance, causes the creation of the form, but always, or at least generally, along lines of growth and action already established.

The thought of a house, if it were impressed upon Formless Substance, might not cause the instantaneous formation of the house; but it would cause the turning of creative energies already working in business and commerce into channels which will result in the building of the house. And if there were no existing channels through which the creative energy could work, then the house would be formed directly from primal substance, without waiting for the slow processes of the organic and inorganic world.

No thought of form can be impressed upon Original Substance without causing the creation of the form.

Mankind is a thinking center, and can originate thought. All the forms that a person fashions with their hands must first exist in thought; a person cannot shape a thing until they have thought that thing. And so far, most people have confined their efforts entirely to the work of "hands"; they apply manual labor to the world of forms, seeking to change or modify those forms already existing. They have never thought of trying to cause the creation of new forms by impressing thoughts directly upon Formless Substance.

When a person has a "thought form", they take material from the forms of nature, and make an image of the form which is in their mind. Humanity, so far, has made little or no effort to co-operate with Formless Intelligence; to work "with God." Humanity has not dreamed that he can "do what he seeth the Father doing." Mankind reshapes and modifies existing forms by manual labor, giving no attention to the question whether things may be produced from Formless Substance by communicating thoughts to it. I propose to prove that any man or woman may do so, and to show how. As our first step, we must lay down three fundamental propositions.

First, we assert that there is one Original Formless substance or energy, from which all things are made. All the seemingly many elements are but different presentations of one element or energy; all the many forms found in organic and inorganic nature are but different shapes, made from the same stuff. And this stuff is thinking stuff; a thought held in it produces the form of the thought. Thought, in thinking substance, produces shapes. Mankind is a thinking center, capable of original thought; if you can communicate thought to original thinking substance, you can cause the creation, or formation, of the thing you think about. To summarize this:-

There is a thinking stuff from which all things are made, and which, in its original state, permeates, penetrates, and fills the interspaces of the universe.
A thought, in this substance, Produces the thing that is imaged by the thought.

16

You can form things in thought, and, by impressing thought upon formless substance, can cause the thing you think about to be created.

You might ask if I can prove these statements; and without going into details, I answer that I can, both by logic, experience, and recent discoveries in Quantum Physics.

Reasoning back from the phenomena of form and thought, I come to one original Thinking Substance; and reasoning forward from this thinking substance, I come to Mankind's power to cause the formation of the things they think about.

I have said that people get rich by doing things in a certain way; and in order to do so, people must become able to **think in a certain way.**

A person's way of doing things is the direct result of the way they think about things.

To do things in a way you want to do them, you will have to acquire the ability to think the way you want to think; this is the first step toward getting rich. *(See the special bonus book, "See Appendix B for meditations exercises to help control your mind)*

To think what you want to think is to think TRUTH, regardless of appearances.

Everyone has the natural and inherent power to think what they wants to think, but it requires far more effort to do so than it does to think the thoughts which are suggested by appearances, or to fall back on the "mental loops" we have become accustomed to. To think according to appearance or habit is easy; to think truth regardless of appearances and to overcome habit is hard, and requires the expenditure of more power than any other work you will be called upon to perform.

There is no work from which most people shrink, as that of disciplined thought; it is the hardest work in the world. This is especially true when truth is contrary to appearances. Every appearance in the visible world tends to produce a corresponding form in the mind; and this can only be prevented by holding the thought of the TRUTH.

To look upon the appearance of disease will produce the form of disease in your own mind, and ultimately in your body, unless you hold the thought of the truth, that there is no disease; it is only an appearance, and the reality is health.

To look upon the appearances of poverty will produce corresponding forms in your own mind, unless you hold to the truth that there is no poverty; there is only abundance.

To think health when surrounded by the appearance of disease, or to think riches when in the midst of apparent poverty, requires discipline; but the person who acquires this discipline becomes a MASTER MIND. They can conquer fate; they can have what they want. This discipline can only be acquired by getting hold of this basic fact; that behind all appearances, there is one Thinking Substance, from which and by which all things are made.

Then we must grasp the truth that every thought held in this substance becomes a form, and that you can so impress your thoughts upon it, and cause them to take form, and become visible things.

When we realize this, we lose all doubt and fear, for we know that we can create what we want to create; we can get what we want to have, and can become what we want to be. As a first step toward getting rich, you must believe the three fundamental statements given previously in this chapter; and in order to emphasize them, I repeat them here:-

There is a thinking stuff from which all things are made, and which, in its original state, permeates, penetrates, and fills the interspaces of the universe.

A thought, in this substance, Produces the thing that is imaged by the thought.
You can form things in thought, and, by impressing thought upon formless substance, can cause the things thought about to be created.

You must set aside all other concepts of the Universe other than this monistic one, this one based on Quantum Phsyics; and you must dwell upon this until it is fixed in your mind, and has become your habitual thought. Read this over and over again; write it out, fix every word upon your mind, and meditate upon them until you firmly believe what they say. If a doubt comes to you, cast it aside. Do not ask why these things are true, nor speculate as to how they can be true; simply take them on trust. The quantum science of getting rich begins with the absolute acceptance of this faith, which is based on Quantum Physics.

CHAPTER 5- Increasing Life

You must get rid of every last vestige of the old idea that there is a Deity, a God, whose will it is that you should be poor, or whose purpose may be served by keeping you in poverty.

The Intelligent Substance which is All, and in All, and which lives in All and lives in you, is a consciously Living Substance. Being a consciously living substance, It must have the nature and inherent desire of every living intelligence for an increase of life. Every living thing must continually seek for the enlargement of its life, because life, in the mere act of living, must increase itself.

A seed, dropped into the ground, springs into activity, and in the act of living produces a hundred more seeds; life, by living, multiplies itself. It is forever Becoming More; it must do so, if it is to continue to be at all.

Intelligence is under this same necessity for continuous increase. Every thought we think makes it necessary for us to think another thought; consciousness is continually expanding. Every fact we learn leads us to the learning of another fact; knowledge is continually increasing. Every talent we cultivate brings the desire to cultivate another talent; we are subject to the urge of life, seeking expression, which ever drives us on to know more, to do more, and to be more.

In order to know more, do more, and be more we must have more; we must have things to use, for we learn, and do, and become, only by using things. We must get rich, so that we can live more.

The desire for riches is simply the capacity for larger life seeking fulfillment; every desire is the effort of an unexpressed possibility to come into action. It is power seeking to manifest, which causes desire. That which makes you want more money is the same as that which makes the plant grow; it is Life, seeking fuller expression.

The One Living Substance must be subject to this inherent law of all life; it is permeated with the desire to live more; that is why it is under the necessity of creating things. The One Substance desires to live more in you; hence it wants you to have all the things you can use.

It is the desire of "God" that you should get rich. The One Living Substance wants you to get rich, because It can express better through you, if you have plenty of things to use in giving It expression. The One Living Substance can live more in you, if you have unlimited command of the means of life.

The Universe desires you to have everything you want to have.

Nature is friendly to your plans.

Everything is naturally for you.

Make up your mind that this is true.

It is essential, however that *your purpose should harmonize with the purpose that is in All.*

You must want *real life*, not power over others, or the simple pleasure of sensual gratification. Life is the performance of function; and the individual really lives only when he performs every function, physical, mental, and spiritual, of which he is capable, without excess in any.

You do not want to get rich in order to live like a despot or a pig, for the gratification of animal desires; that is not life. But the performance of every physical function is a part of life, and no one lives completely who denies the impulses of the body a normal and healthful expression.

You do not want to get rich solely to enjoy mental pleasures, to get knowledge, to gratify ambition, to outshine others, to be famous, or for power. All these are a legitimate part of life, but the person who lives for the pleasures of the intellect alone will only have a partial life, and they will never be satisfied.

You do not want to get rich solely for the good of others, to lose yourself for the salvation of mankind, to experience the joys of philanthropy and sacrifice. The joys of the soul are only a part of life; and they are no better or nobler than any other part.

You want to get rich in order that you may eat, drink, and be merry when it is time to do these things; in order that you may surround yourself with beautiful things, see distant places, feed your mind, and develop your intellect; in order that you may love mankind and do kind things, and be able to play a good part in helping the World to find Truth. But remember, extreme altruism is no better and no nobler than extreme selfishness; both are mistakes.

Get rid of the idea that "God" wants you to sacrifice yourself for others, and that you can secure his favor by doing so; "God" requires nothing of the kind. What "God" wants is that you make the most of yourself- for yourself, and for others; and *you can help others more by making the most of yourself than in any other way.*

You can make the most of yourself only by getting rich; so it is right and praiseworthy that you should give your first and best thoughts to the work of acquiring wealth.

Remember, however, that the desire of Substance is for all, and its movements must be for more life to all; it cannot be made to work for less life to any, because it is equally in all, seeking riches and life.

Intelligent Substance will make things for you, but it will not take things away from some one else and give them to you. You must get rid of the thought of competition.

You are to create, not to compete for what is already created.

You do not have to take anything away from any one.

You do not have to drive hard bargains.

You do not have to cheat or to take advantage.

You do not need to let anyone work for you for less than they earn.

You do not have to "covet" the property of others, or to look at it with jealousy; no one has anything you cannot have, and without taking what they have away.

You are to become a creator, not a competitor; you are going to get what you want, but in such a way that when you get it, every other person will have more than they have now too.

I am aware that there are people who get a vast amount of money by doing the direct opposite, and if I might add a word of explanation; these are people of the "plutocratic" type, the corporate CEO and politician types, who become very rich purely by their extraordinary drive and ability on the plane of competition; sometimes they unconsciously relate themselves to Substance in its greater purposes and movements for the general human upbuilding through industrial evolution. Rockefeller, Bill Gates, Morgan Stanley, etc have been the unconscious agents of the Supreme in the necessary work of systematizing and organizing productive industry; and in the end, their work will contribute immensely toward increased life for all. Once they have organized production, they *will soon be succeeded by the agents of the multitude, who will organize the machinery of distribution.*

The multi-Billionaires are like the dinosaurs; they play a necessary part in the evolutionary process, but the same Power which produces them will eventually dispose of them. And you might bear in mind that they have never been really rich; a look at their private lives often shows they have really been the most abject and wretched of the poor, in spirit and happiness, at least.

Riches secured on the competitive plane are never satisfactory and permanent; they are yours today, and another's tomorrow. Remember, if you are to become rich in a quantum and certain way, you must rise entirely above competitive thought. You must never think for a moment that the supply is limited. Just as soon as you begin to think that all the money is being "cornered" and controlled by corporations, and that you must work to get laws passed to stop the corporate takeover; in that moment, you drop into the competitive mind, and your power to cause creation is gone for the time being; and what is worse, you will probably arrest the creative movements you have already set in motion!

Know that there are countless billions of dollars' worth of gold in the mountains of the earth, not yet brought to light; and know that if there were not, more would be created from Thinking Substance to supply your needs.

Know that the money you need will come, even if it is necessary for a thousand men to be led to the discovery of new gold mines tomorrow.

Never look at the visible supply; look always at the limitless riches in Formless Substance, and KNOW that they are coming to you as fast as you can receive and use them. Nobody, by cornering the visible supply, can prevent you from getting what is yours.

So never allow yourself to think for an instant that all the best building spots will be taken before you get ready to build your house, unless you hurry. Never worry about the corporations, and fear they will soon own the entire Earth. Never be afraid that you will lose what you want, because some other person "beats you to it." That cannot possibly happen; you are not seeking any thing that is possessed by anybody else; you are causing what you want to be created from Formless Substance, and the supply is without limits. Stick to the formulated statement:-

There is a thinking stuff from which all things are made, and which, in its original state, permeates, penetrates, and fills the interspaces of the universe.
A thought, in this substance, produces the thing that is imaged by the thought.
You can form things in thought, and, by impressing thought upon formless substance, can cause the things thought about to be created.

CHAPTER 6- How Riches Come to You

When I say that you do not have to drive hard bargains, I don't mean you do not have to drive any bargains, or that you are above the necessity for having any dealings with your fellow man or woman. I mean that you will not need to deal with them unfairly; you do not have to get something for nothing, *but can give to everyone more than you take.*

You cannot give everyone more in cash market value than you take, but you can give more in use value than the cash value of the thing you take. The computer image of this eBook, or the paper, ink, and other material in this paperback may not be worth the money you paid for it; but if the ideas bring you thousands of dollars, you have been given a great use value for a small cash value.

24

Let's suppose that I own a painting by one of the great artists, which is worth thousands of dollars. I take it to the Amazon Rain Forest, and by "salesmanship" induce an indigenous people to give a bundle of healing herbs worth $ 500 for it. Even though they may have received a greater "cash value", I have really wronged them- they have no use for the painting; it has no "use value", it will not add to their life.

But suppose I give them high quality garden tools worth $50 for the herbs; then they may have made a good bargain. They have a use for garden tools; they can use them to grow more herbs and much food, and it will make their work easier, allowing them to cultivate more, and provide themselves a better lifestyle; it will add to their life in every way; it will make them rich.

When you rise from the competitive to the creative plane, you can scan your business transactions very strictly, and if you are selling anyone anything which does not add more to their life than the thing they give you in exchange, you can afford to stop it. You do not have to beat anybody in business. And if you are in a business which does beat people, get out of it at once!

Give everyone more in use value than you take from them in cash value; then you are adding to the life of the world with every business transaction.

If you have people working for you, you must take from them more in cash value than you pay them in wages; but you can so organize your business that it will be filled with the principle of advancement, so that each employee who wishes to do so, may advance a little every day. You can make your business do for your employees what this book is doing for you.

And finally, because you are to cause the creation of your riches from Formless Substance, which permeates all your environment, it does not follow that they are to take shape from the atmosphere and come into being before your eyes. If you want a car, for instance, I do not mean that you are to impress the thought of a car on Thinking Substance until the car is formed without hands, right in your driveway. But if you want a car, hold the mental image of it with the most positive certainty that it is being made, or is on its way to you. After once forming the thought, have the most absolute and unquestioning faith that the car is coming; never think of it, or speak of it, in any other way, than as being sure to arrive. Claim it as already yours.

It will be brought to you by the power of the Supreme Intelligence, acting upon the minds of people. If you live in Maine, it may be that a man will be brought from Texas or Japan to engage in some business transaction, which will result in your getting what you want. If so, the whole matter will be as much to that person's advantage as it is to yours.

Do not forget for a moment that the Thinking Substance is through all, in all, communicating with all, and can influence all. The desire of Thinking Substance for fuller life and better living has caused the creation of all the cars already made; and it can cause the creation of millions more, and will, whenever people set it in motion by desire and faith, and by acting in a certain way.

You can certainly have a car; and it is just as certain that you can have any other thing you want, which you will use for the advancement of your own life, and the lives of others. You need not hesitate about asking largely; "it is your Father's pleasure to give you the kingdom," said Jesus.

Original Substance wants to live all that is possible in you, and wants you to have all that you can or will use for the living of the most abundant life.

If you fix upon your consciousness the fact that the desire you feel for the possession of riches is one with the desire of Omnipotence for more complete expression, your faith becomes invincible.

26

Once I saw a little boy sitting at a piano, vainly trying to bring harmony out of the keys; and I saw that he was frustrated by his inability to play real music. I asked him the cause of his frustration, and he answered, "I can feel the music in me, but I can't make my hands go right." The music in him was the URGE of Original Substance, containing all the possibilities of life; all that there is of music was seeking expression through the child.

God, Goddess, the One Substance, is trying to live, and do, and enjoy things through humanity. It is saying "I want hands to build wonderful structures, to play divine harmonies, to paint glorious pictures; I want feet to run my errands, eyes to see my beauties, tongues to tell mighty truths and to sing marvelous songs," and so on.

All that there is of possibility is seeking expression through people. The Universe wants those who can play music to have pianos and every other instrument, and to have the means to cultivate their talents to the fullest extent; It wants those who can appreciate beauty to be able to surround themselves with beautiful things; It wants those who can discern truth to have every opportunity to travel and observe; It wants those who can appreciate dress to be beautifully clothed, and those who can appreciate good food to be luxuriously fed.

It wants all these things because It enjoys and appreciates them; it is "God" who wants to play, and sing, and enjoy beauty, and proclaim truth and wear fine clothes, and eat good food. "it is God that worketh in you to will and to do," said Paul.

The desire you feel for riches is the Infinite, seeking to express Itself in you, as It sought to find expression in the little boy at the piano.

So you need not hesitate to ask largely.

Your part is to focalize and express the desire to "God".

This is a difficult point with most people; they retain something of the old idea that poverty and self-sacrifice are pleasing to God. They look upon poverty as a part of the plan, a necessity of nature. They have the idea that God has finished His work, and made all that He can make, and that the majority of men must stay poor because there is not enough to go around. They hold to so much of this erroneous thought that they feel ashamed to ask for wealth; they try not to want more than a very modest amount, just enough to make them comfortable.

I recall the case of one person who was told he must get in mind a clear picture of the things he desired, so that the creative thought of them might be impressed on Formless Substance. He was a very poor man, living in a rented room, and having only what he earned from day to day; and he could not grasp the fact that all wealth was his. So, after thinking about it, he decided that he might reasonably ask for a new rug for the floor of his room, and an electric heater to heat the room during the Winter. Following the instructions given in this book, he got these things in a few months; and then it dawned on him that he had not asked for enough! He went through the neighborhood where he lived, and worked out an idea for an apartment he'd like to have; he mentally added a bay window here, and a skylight there, until it was complete in his mind as his ideal home.

Holding the whole picture in his mind, he began living in a certain way, and moving toward what he wanted; and he owns a condominium now, and is remodeling it into the form of his mental image. And now, with a still larger faith, he is going on to get greater things. It has been unto him according to his faith, and it is so with you, and with all of us.

CHAPTER 7- Gratitude

The examples given in the last chapter will have conveyed to you the fact that the first step toward getting rich is to convey the idea of what you want to the Formless Substance.

This is true, and you will see that in order to do so, it becomes necessary to relate yourself to the Formless Intelligence in a harmonious way. This harmonious relationship is a matter of such primary and vital importance, that I will give some discussion to it here, and give you instructions which, if you follow them, will be certain to bring you into perfect unity of mind with "God", the Intelligent Substance.

The whole process of mental adjustment and atonement can be summed up in one word, GRATITUDE.

First, you believe that there is one Intelligent Substance, from which all things proceed; second, you believe that this Substance gives you everything you desire; and third, you relate yourself to it by a feeling of deep and profound gratitude.

Many people who order their lives rightly in all other ways are kept in poverty by their lack of gratitude. Having received one gift, they cut the wires which connect them with It by failing to make acknowledgment.

It is easy to understand that the nearer we live to the source of wealth, the more wealth we shall receive; and it is easy also to understand that the soul that is always grateful lives in closer touch with "God" than the one which never looks to It in thankful acknowledgment.

The more gratefully we fix our minds on the Supreme when good things come to us, the more good things we will receive, and the more rapidly they will come; and the reason is simply that the mental attitude of gratitude draws the mind into closer touch with the source from which the blessings come.

If it's a novel thought to you that gratitude brings your whole mind into closer harmony with the creative energies of the Universe, consider it, and you will see that it's true. The good things you already have come to you along the line of obedience to certain laws. Gratitude will lead your mind out along the ways by which things come; and it will keep you in close harmony with creative thought and prevent you from falling into competitive thought.

Gratitude alone can keep you looking toward the All, and prevent you from falling into the error of thinking of the supply as limited; and to do that would be fatal to your hopes. There is a Law of Gratitude, and it is absolutely necessary that you should observe the law, if you are to get the results you seek. The law of gratitude is the natural principle that action and reaction are always equal, and in opposite directions. The grateful outreaching of your mind in thankful praise to the Supreme *is a liberation or expenditure of energy; it cannot fail to reach that to which it is addressed, and the reaction is an instantaneous movement towards you.*

"Draw nigh unto God, and He will draw nigh unto you." That is a statement of psychological truth.

And if your gratitude is strong and constant, the reaction in Formless Substance will be strong and continuous; the movement of the things you want will be always toward you. Notice the grateful attitude that Jesus took; how He always seems to be saying, "I thank Thee, Father, that Thou hearest me." You cannot exercise much energy without gratitude; for it is gratitude that keeps you connected with Energy.

But the value of gratitude does not consist solely in getting you more blessings in the future. Without gratitude, you can't keep from a dissatisfied thought regarding things the way they are. The moment you permit your mind to dwell with dissatisfaction upon things as they are, you begin to lose ground. You fix attention upon the common, the ordinary, the poor, the squalid and the mean; and your mind takes the form of these things. Then you will transmit these forms or mental images to the Formless, and the common, the poor, the squalid, and mean will come to you.

To permit your mind to dwell upon the inferior is to become inferior and to surround yourself with inferior things.

30

On the other hand, to fix your attention on the best is to surround yourself with the best, and to become the best.

The Creative Power within us makes us into the image of that to which we give our attention. We are Thinking Substance, and thinking substance always takes the form of that which it thinks about.

The grateful mind is constantly fixed upon the best; therefore it tends to become the best; it takes the form or character of the best, and will receive the best.

Also, faith is born of gratitude. The grateful mind continually expects good things, and expectation becomes faith. The reaction of gratitude upon one's own mind produces faith; and every outgoing wave of grateful thanksgiving increases faith. The person who has no feeling of gratitude cannot long retain a living faith; and *without a living faith you cannot get rich by the creative method,* as we shall see in the following chapters.

It is necessary, then, to cultivate the habit of being grateful for every good thing that comes to you; and to give thanks continuously. And because all things have contributed to your advancement (even situations that appear bad), you should include all things in your gratitude.

Do not waste time thinking or talking about the shortcomings or wrong doings of corporations. Their organization of the world has made your opportunity; all you get really comes to you because of them. Do not rage against the government and corrupt politicians; if it were not for the government and the politicians, we would fall into anarchy, and your opportunity for wealth would be nil!

Intelligent Substance has worked a long time and very patiently to bring us up to where we are in industry and government, and It is going right on with It's work. There is not the least doubt that It will do away with corporations and politicians as soon as they can be spared; but in the meantime, consider that they are all very good. Remember that they are all helping to arrange the lines of transmission along which your riches will come to you, and be grateful to them all. This will bring you into harmonious relations with the good in everything, and the good in everything will move toward you.

CHAPTER 8- Thinking in a Certain Way

Turn back to chapter 6 and read again the story of the man who formed a mental image of his house, and you will get a fair idea of the initial step toward getting rich. You must form a clear and definite mental picture of what you want; you cannot transmit an idea unless you have it yourself.

You must have it before you can give it; and many people fail to impress Thinking Substance because they have themselves only a vague and misty concept of the things they want to do, to have, or to become.

It is not enough that you should have a general desire for wealth "to do good with"; everybody has that desire.

It is not enough that you should have a wish to travel, see things, live more, etc. Everyone has those desires too. If you were going to send an e-mail to a friend, you would not send the letters of the alphabet, and let them construct the message for themselves; nor would you take words at random from the dictionary. You would send a coherent sentence; one which meant something. When you try to impress your wants upon Substance, remember that it must be done by a coherent statement; you must know what you want, and be definite. You can never get rich, or start the creative energy into action, by sending out unformed longings, wishes and vague desires.

Go over your desires just as the man went over his house; see just what you want, and get as clear mental picture as you can. That clear mental picture you must have continually in mind (*without obsession or neediness, see Appendix B)* just as the sailor has in mind the port toward which he is sailing the ship; you must keep your face toward it all the time.

Spend as much of your leisure time as you can in contemplating your vision- no one needs to practice concentrating on a thing which they really want. *(What requires practice is keeping out the things you don't want from intruding into your mind! For some tips and exercises that can help, see Appendix B.)* And unless you really *want* to get rich, so that the desire is strong enough to hold your thoughts to that purpose, as the magnetic pole holds the needle of the compass, it will hardly be worth while for you to try to carry out the instructions given in this book. The methods herein are for people whose desire for riches is strong enough to overcome mental laziness, and make them work. The more clear and definite you make your picture, and the more you dwell upon it, bringing out all the delightful details, the stronger your desire will be; and the stronger your desire, the easier it will be to hold your mind fixed upon the picture of what you want.

Something more is necessary, however, than merely to see the picture clearly. If that's all you do, you are only a daydreamer, and will have little or no power for accomplishment. Behind your clear vision must be the purpose to realize it; to bring it out in tangible expression. And behind this purpose must be an invincible and unwavering FAITH that the thing is already yours; that it is "at hand" and you have only to take possession of it.

Live in the new house, mentally, until it takes form around you physically. In the mental realm, enter at once into full enjoyment of the things you want. "Whatsoever things ye ask for when ye pray, believe that ye receive them, and ye shall have them," said Jesus.

See the things you want as if they were actually around you all the time; see yourself as owning and using them. Make use of them in

33

imagination, just as you will use them when they are your tangible possessions. Dwell upon your mental picture until it is clear and distinct, and then take the Mental Attitude of Ownership toward everything in that picture. Take possession of it, in mind, in the full faith that it is actually yours. Hold to this mental ownership; do not waiver for an instant in the faith that it is real. And remember what was said in a proceeding chapter about gratitude; be as thankful for it all the time, as you expect to be when it has taken form. The person who can sincerely thank God for the things which they own only in imagination, has real faith. They will get rich; they will cause the creation of whatever they want.

You do not need to pray repeatedly for things you want; it is not necessary to tell Intelligent Substance about it every day. "Use not vain repetitions as the heathen do," said Jesus said to his pupils, "for your Father knoweth the ye have need of these things before ye ask Him." Your part is to intelligently formulate your desire for the things which make for a larger life, and to get these desires arranged into a coherent whole; and then to impress this Whole Desire upon the Formless Substance, which has the power and the will to bring you what you want. You do not make this impression by repeating strings of words; you make it by holding the vision with unshakable PURPOSE to attain it, and with steadfast FAITH that you do attain it. The answer to prayer is not according to your faith while you are talking, but according to your faith while you are working.

You cannot impress the mind of God by having a special Sabbath day set apart to tell Him what you want, and then forgetting Him during the rest of the week. You cannot impress Him by having special hours to go into your church and pray, if you then dismiss the matter from your mind until Sunday comes again.

Oral prayer is good, and has its effect, especially on yourself, in clarifying your vision and strengthening your faith; but it is not your oral petitions which get you what you want. In order to get rich you do not need a "sweet hour of prayer"; you need to "pray without ceasing." And by prayer I mean holding steadily to your vision, with the purpose to cause its creation in solid form, and the faith that you are doing so.

"Believe that ye receive them."

The whole matter turns on receiving, once you have clearly formed your vision. When you have formed it, it is good to make an oral statement, addressing the Supreme in reverent prayer; and from that moment you must, in mind, receive what you ask for. Live in the new house, wear the designer clothes, drive the car, go on the vacation, and confidently plan for greater journeys. Think and speak of all the things you have asked for in terms of actual present ownership. Imagine an environment, and a financial condition exactly as you want them, and live all the time in that imaginary environment and financial condition. Mind, however, that you do not do this as a mere day dreamer; hold to the FAITH that the imaginary is being realized, and to the PURPOSE to realize it. Remember that it is faith and purpose in the use of the imagination which make the difference between the metaphysician and the dreamer. And having learned this fact, it is here that you must learn the proper use of the Will.

CHAPTER 9- How to Use the Will

To set about getting rich in a scientific way, you do not try to apply your will power to anything outside of yourself. Your have no right to do so, anyway. It is wrong to apply your will to other men and women, in order to get them to do what you want.

It is as flagrantly wrong to coerce people by mental power as it is to coerce them by physical power. If compelling people by physical force to do things for you reduces them to slavery, compelling them by mental means accomplishes exactly the same thing; the only difference is in methods. If taking things from people by physical force is robbery, them taking things by mental force is robbery too; there is no difference in principle.

You have no right to use your will power upon another person, even "for his own good"; for you do not know what is "for his good". The quantum science of getting rich does not require you to apply power or force to any other person, in any way whatsoever. There is not the slightest necessity for doing so; indeed, any attempt to use your will upon others will only tend to defeat your purpose.

You don't need to apply your will to things, in order to compel them to come to you. That would simply be trying to coerce the Supreme, and would be foolish and useless, as well as irreverent. You do not have to compel Formless Substance to give you good things, any more than you have to use your will power to make the sun rise. You do not have to use your will power to conquer an unfriendly deity, or to make stubborn and rebellious forces do your bidding.

Substance is friendly to you, and is more anxious to give you what you want than you are to get it. *To get rich, you need only to use your will power upon yourself. When you know what to think and do, then you must use your will to compel yourself to think and do the right things.* That is the legitimate use of the will in getting what you want- to use it in holding yourself to the right course. Use your will to keep yourself thinking and acting in a certain way.

Do not try to project your will, or your thoughts, or your mind out into space, to "act" on things or people. Keep your mind at home; it can accomplish more there than elsewhere. Use your mind to form a mental image of what you want, and to hold that vision with faith and purpose; and use your will to keep your mind working in the right way.

The more steady and continuous your faith and purpose, the more rapidly you will get rich, because you will make only POSITIVE impressions upon Substance; and you will not neutralize or offset them by negative impressions. The picture of your desires, held with faith and purpose, is taken up by the Formless, and permeates it to great distances- throughout the universe, for all I know! As this impression spreads, all things are set moving toward its realization; every living thing, every inanimate object, and the things yet uncreated, are stirred toward bringing into being that which you want. All energy begins to be exerted in that direction; all things begin to move toward you. The minds of people, everywhere, are influenced toward doing the things necessary to the fulfilling of your desires; and they work for you, unconsciously.

But you can check all this by starting a negative impression in the Formless Substance. Doubt or disbelief is as certain to start a movement away from you as faith and purpose are to start one toward you. It is by not understanding this, that most people who try to make use of "mental science" fail. Every hour and moment you spend in giving in to doubts and fears, every hour you spend worrying, every hour in which your soul is possessed by disbelief, sets a current away from you in the whole domain of Intelligent Substance. All the promises are unto them that believe, and unto them only. Notice how insistent Jesus was upon this point of belief; and now you know the reason why.

Since belief is all important, it behooves you to guard your thoughts; and as your beliefs will be shaped to a very great extent by the things you observe and think about, it is important that you should command your own attention. And here the will comes into use; for it is by your will that you determine upon what things your attention shall be fixed. If you want to become rich, you must not make a study of poverty. Things are not brought into being by thinking about their opposites. Health is never to be attained by studying disease and thinking about disease; righteousness is not to be promoted by studying sin and thinking about sin; and no one ever got rich by studying poverty and thinking about poverty.

Medicine as a science of disease has increased disease; religion as a science of sin has promoted sin, and economics as a study of poverty will fill the world with poverty.

Do not talk about poverty; do not investigate it, do not concern yourself with it. Never mind what its causes are; you have nothing to do with them.

What concerns you is the cure.

Do not spend your time in charitable work, or social movements; all charity only tends to perpetuate the conditions it aims to eradicate. I don't say you should be hard hearted or unkind, and refuse to hear the cry of the needy; but you must not try to eradicate poverty in any of the conventional ways. Put poverty behind you, and put all that pertains to it behind you, and "make good."

Get rich; that is the best way you can help the poor.

And you can't hold the mental image that will make you rich if you fill your mind with pictures of poverty. Do not read stories or watch shows which give circumstantial accounts of the horrors of the ghettos, or the wretchedness of the Third World. Do not read anything which fills your mind with gloomy images of want and suffering.

You cannot help the poor in the least by knowing about these things; and the wide-spread knowledge of them does not tend to do away with poverty. What tends to do away with poverty is not getting pictures of poverty into your mind, but getting pictures of wealth into the minds of the poor. You are not deserting the poor in their misery when you refuse to allow your mind to be filled with pictures of that misery.

Poverty can be done away with, not by increasing the number of well to do people who think about poverty, but by increasing the number of poor people who purpose, with faith, is to get rich.

38

The poor do not need charity; they need inspiration. Charity only sends them food stamps to keep them alive in their misery, or gives them an entertainment to make them forget for an hour or two; but inspiration will cause them to rise out of their misery. If you want to help the poor, demonstrate to them that they can become rich, and prove it by getting rich yourself.

The only way in which poverty will ever be banished from this world is by getting a large and constantly increasing number of people to practice the teachings of this book. People must be taught to become rich by creation, not by competition. Everyone who becomes rich by competition throws down the ladder by which they rise, and keeps others down; but everyone who gets rich by creation opens a way for thousands to follow, and inspires them to do so.

You are not showing hardness of heart or an unfeeling character when you refuse to pity poverty, see poverty, read about poverty, or think or talk about it, or to listen to those who do talk about it. Use your will power to keep your mind OFF the subject of poverty, and to keep it fixed with faith and purpose ON the vision of what you want.

CHAPTER 10- Further Use of the Will

You cannot retain a true and clear vision of wealth if you are constantly turning your attention to opposing pictures, whether they be external or imaginary. Do not tell of your past financial woes, don't think of them at all. Do not tell of the poverty of your parents, or the hardships of your early life; to do any of these things is to mentally class yourself with the poor for the time being, and it will certainly check the movement of things moving in your direction.

"Let the dead bury their dead," as Jesus said.

Put poverty and all things that pertain to poverty completely behind you.

You have accepted a certain theory of the Universe as being correct, and are resting all your hopes of happiness on its being correct; and what can you gain by giving in to conflicting theories? Do not read religious books which tell you that the world is coming to an end; and don't read pessimistic philosophers who tell you that the world going to Hell. The world is not going to the Hell; it is growing into Heaven.

It is wonderful Becoming.

True, there may be a lot of things existing which are terrible; but what is the use of studying them when they are passing away, and when the study of them only tends to check their passing and keep them with us? Why give time and attention to things which are being removed by evolutionary growth, when you can hasten their removal only by promoting the evolutionary growth as far as your part goes?

No matter how horrible the seeming conditions, you waste your time and destroy your own chances by considering them. You should interest yourself in the world's becoming rich. Think of the riches the world is coming into, instead of the poverty it is growing out of; and bear in mind that the only way in which you can assist the world in growing rich is by growing rich yourself, through the creative method, not the competitive one. Give your attention wholly to riches; ignore poverty.

Whenever you think or speak of those who are poor, think and speak of them as those who are becoming rich, as those who are to be congratulated rather than pitied. Then they and others will catch the inspiration, and begin to search for the way out.

Because I say that you are to give your whole time, mind and thought to riches, it does not follow that you are to be greedy or selfish. To become really rich is the noblest aim you can have in life, for it includes everything else.

40

On the competitive plane, the struggle to get rich is a Godless scramble for power over others; but when we come into the creative mind, all this is changed. All that is possible in the way of greatness and soul unfoldment, of service and lofty endeavor, comes by way of getting rich; all is made possible by the use of things.

If you lack for physical health, you will find that the attainment of it is conditional on your getting rich. Only those who are emancipated from financial worry, and who have the means to live a care-free existence, and follow healthy practices, can have and retain health- and that takes money!

Moral and spiritual greatness is possible only to those who are above the competitive battle for existence; and only those who are becoming rich on the plane of creative thought are free from the degrading influences of competition. If your heart is set on domestic happiness, remember that love flourishes best where there is refinement, a high level of thought, and freedom from corrupting influences; and these are to be found only where riches are attained by the exercise of creative thought, without strife or rivalry.

You can aim at nothing so great or noble, I repeat, as to become rich by the creative method; and you must fix your attention upon your mental picture of riches, to the exclusion of all that may tend to dim or obscure the vision.

You must learn to see the underlying TRUTH in all things; you must see beneath all seemingly wrong conditions, and see the Great One Life ever moving forward toward fuller expression and more complete happiness. It is the truth that there is no such thing as poverty; that there is only wealth. Some people remain in poverty because they are ignorant of the fact that there is wealth for them; and these can best be taught by showing them the way to affluence in your own personal practice.

Others are poor because, while they feel there is a way out, they are too intellectually lazy to put forth the mental effort to find that way and travel it; and for these the very best thing you can do is to arouse their desire by showing them the happiness that comes from being rightly rich.

Others are poor because, while they have some notion of quantum science, they have become so swamped and lost in the maze of metaphysical and occult theories that they do not know which road to take. They try a mixture of many systems and fail in all. Again, the very best thing to do is to show the right way in your own person and practice; an ounce of doing things is worth a pound of theorizing.

The very best thing you can do for the whole world is to make the most of yourself. You can serve God and man in no more effective way than by getting rich; that is, if you get rich by the creative method and not by the competitive one.

Another thing- we assert that this book gives the principles of the quantum science of getting rich; and if that is true, you do not need to read any other book on the subject. This may sound egotistical, but consider: there can only be one shortest distance between two points. There is only one way to think quantum scientifically, and that is to think in the way that leads to the most direct and simple route to the goal. No one has yet formulated a briefer or less complex "system" than the one set forth here; it has been stripped of all non-essentials. When you start this, lay all other systems aside; put them out of your mind altogether.

Read this book every day; print it out, or better yet, buy the paperback and keep it with you; commit it to memory, and do not think about other "systems" and theories. If you do, you will have doubts, and be uncertain and wavering in your thought; and then you will begin to make mistakes. After you have made good and become rich, you may study other systems, but until you are quite sure you have gained what

42

you want, do not read anything on this subject but this book. And read only the most optimistic comments on the world's news; those in harmony with your picture.

There is a thinking stuff from which all things are made, and which, in its original state, permeates, penetrates, and fills the interspaces of the universe.

A thought, in this substance, Produces the thing that is imaged by the thought.

A person can form things in thought, and, by impressing thought upon formless substance, can cause the thing thought about to be created.

In order to do this, you must pass from the competitive to the creative mind; you must form a clear mental picture of the things you want, and hold this picture in thought with the fixed PURPOSE to get what you want, and the unwavering FAITH that you will get what you want, closing your mind against all that may tend to shake your purpose, dim your vision, or quench your faith.

And in addition to all this, we shall now see that you must live and act in a certain way.

CHAPTER 11- Acting in a Certain Way

Thought is the creative power, or the impelling force, which causes the creative power to act; thinking in a certain way will bring riches to you, but you must not rely on thought alone, paying no attention to personal actions. That's where many metaphysical "thinkers" meet with failure; they fail to connect thought with personal action.

We have not yet reached the stage of development, supposing that such a stage is possible, in which man can create directly from

Formless Substance without nature's processes, or the work of human hands; people must not only think, but personal action must supplement thought.

By thought, you can cause the gold in the heart of the mountain to be impelled towards you; but it will not mine itself, refine itself, coin itself, and come rolling along the roads seeking its way into your pocket!

Under the impelling power of the Supreme Spirit, affairs will be so ordered that someone will be led to mine the gold for you; business transactions will be directed so that the gold will be brought toward you, and you must so arrange your own business affairs and your life so that you may be able to receive it when it comes. Your thought makes all things, animate and inanimate, work to bring you what you want; but your personal activity must be such that you can rightly receive what you want when it reaches you. You are not to take it as charity, nor to steal it; you must give everyone more in use value than they give you in cash value.

The scientific use of thought consists in forming a clear and distinct mental image of what you want; in holding fast to the purpose of getting what you want; and in realizing with grateful faith that you do get what you want.

Do not try to 'project' your thought in any mysterious or occult way, with the idea of having it go out and do things for you; that is wasted effort, and will weaken your ability to think sanely.

The action of thought in getting rich is fully explained in the preceding chapters; your faith and purpose positively impress your vision upon Formless Substance, which has THE SAME DESIRE FOR MORE LIFE THAT YOU HAVE; and this vision, received from you, sets all the creative forces at work IN AND THROUGH THEIR REGULAR CHANNELS OF ACTION, but directed toward you.

It is not your part to guide or supervise the creative process; all you have to do with that is to retain your vision, stick to your purpose, and maintain your faith and gratitude. But you must act in a certain way, so you can receive what is yours when it comes to you; so that you can meet the things you have in your picture, and put them in their proper place as they arrive.

You can really see the truth of this. When things reach you, they will be in the hands of other people, who will ask an equivalent for them. And you can only get what is yours by giving the other person what is their due.

Your pocketbook is not going to be transformed into a winning lottery ticket. This is the crucial point, right here, where thought and personal action must be combined. There are many people who, consciously or unconsciously, set the creative forces in action by the strength and persistence of their desires, but who remain poor because they do not provide for the reception of the thing they want when it comes.

By thought, the thing you want is brought to you; by action you receive it. Whatever your action is to be, it is evident that you must act NOW. You cannot act in the past, and it is essential to the clearness of your mental vision that you dismiss the past from your mind. You cannot act in the future, for the future is not here yet.

Because you're not in the right business, or the right environment now, don't think that you must postpone action until you can get into the right business or environment. And don't spend time in the present thinking about the best course of action in possible future emergencies; have faith in your ability to meet any emergency when it comes.
If you act in the present with your mind on the future, your present action will be with a divided mind, and will not be effective.

Put your whole mind into present action.

Do not give your creative impulse to Original Substance, and then sit down and wait for results; if you do, you will never get them. Act now.

There is never any time but now, and there never will be any time but now. If you are ever to begin making ready for the reception of what you want, you must begin now. And your action, whatever it is, must most likely be in your present business or employment, and must be upon the persons and things in your present environment.

You cannot act where you are not; you cannot act where you have been, and you cannot act where you are going to be; you can act only where you are.

Do not bother as to whether yesterday's work was well done or ill done;

do today's

work well.

Do not try to do tomorrow's work now; there will be plenty of time to do

that when you

get to it.

Do not try, by occult or mystical means, to act on people or things that are

out of your reach.

Do not wait for a change of environment before you act; get a change of

environment by action.

You can so act upon the environment in which you are now, as to cause yourself to be transferred to a better environment. Hold with faith and purpose the vision of yourself in the better environment, but act upon your present environment with all your heart, and with all your strength, and with all your mind.

Do not spend any time in day dreaming or castle building; hold to the one vision of what you want, and act NOW.

Do not go out seeking new things to do, or some remarkable action to perform as a first step toward getting rich. It is probable that your actions, at least for some time, will be those you have been performing for some time; but you are to begin now to perform these actions in the certain way, which will surely make you rich. If you are engaged in some business, and feel that it's not the right one for you, don't wait until you get into the right business before you begin to act.

Do not feel discouraged, or sit down and lament because you are misplaced. No one was ever so misplaced but that they could not find the right place, and no one ever became so involved in the wrong business but that they could get into the right business.

Hold the vision of yourself in the right business, with the purpose of getting into it, and the faith that you will get into it, and are getting into it; but ACT in your present business. Use your present business as the means of getting a better one, and use your present environment as the means of getting into a better one. Your vision of the right business, if held with faith and purpose, will cause the Supreme to move the right business toward you; and your action, if performed in the certain way, will cause you to move toward the business.

If you are an employee, and feel you must change places in order to get what you want, do not "project" your thought into space and rely upon it to get you another job. It will probably fail to do so. Hold the vision of yourself in the job you want, while you ACT with faith and purpose on the job you have, and you will certainly get the job you want. Your vision and faith will set the creative force in motion to bring it toward you, and your action will cause the forces in your own environment to move you toward the place you want. In closing this chapter, we will add another statement to our syllabus:

There is a thinking stuff from which all things are made, and which, in its original state, permeates, penetrates, and fills the interspaces of the universe.
A thought, in this substance, Produces the thing that is imaged by the thought.

A person can form things in thought, and, by impressing thought upon
formless substance, can cause the thing thought about to be created.
In order to do this, you must pass from the competitive to the creative
mind; you must form a clear mental picture of the things you want, and
hold this picture in thoughts with the fixed PURPOSE to get what you
want, and the unwavering FAITH that you do get what you want, closing
your mind to all that may tend to shake your purpose, dim your vision, or
quench your faith.
That you may receive what you want when it comes, you must act NOW
upon the people and things in your present environment.

CHAPTER 12- Efficient Action

You must use your thought as directed in previous chapters, and begin to do what you can do where you are; and you must do ALL that you can do where you are.

You can advance only by being larger than your present place; and no one is larger than their present place who leaves undone any of the work pertaining to that place. The world is advanced only by those who more than fill their present places.

If no one quite filled their present place, you can see that there must be a going backward in everything. Those who do not quite fill their present place are dead weight upon society, government, commerce, and industry; they must be carried along by others at a great expense. The progress of the world is held back only by those who do not fill the places they are holding; they belong to a former age and a lower stage or plane of life, and their tendency is toward degeneration. No society could advance if everyone was smaller than their place; social evolution is guided by the law of physical and mental evolution. In the animal world, evolution is caused by excess of life.

When an organism has more life than can be expressed in the functions of its own plane, it develops the organs of a higher plane, and a new species is originated. There never would have been new species had there not been organisms which more than filled their places. The law is exactly the same for you; your getting rich depends upon your applying this principle to your own affairs.

Every day is either a successful day or a day of failure; and it is the successful days which get you what you want. If everyday is a failure, you can never get rich; while if every day is a success, you cannot fail to get rich.

If there is something that may be done today, and you do not do it, you have failed in so far as that thing is concerned; and the consequences may be more disastrous than you imagine.

You can't foresee the results of even the most trivial act; you do not know the workings of all the forces that have been set moving in your behalf. Much may be depending on your doing some simple act; it may be the very thing which is to open the door of opportunity to very great possibilities. You can never know all the combinations which Supreme Intelligence is making for you in the world of things and human affairs; your neglect or failure to do some small thing may cause a long delay in getting what you want.

Do, every day, ALL that can be done that day.

There is, however, a limitation or qualification of the above that you must take into account. You are not to overwork, nor to rush blindly into your business in order to do the greatest possible number of things in the shortest possible time. You are not to try to do tomorrow's work today, nor to do a week's work in a day.

It is really not the number of things you do, but the EFFICIENCY of each separate action that counts.

Every act is, in itself, either a success or a failure.

Every act is, in itself, either effective or inefficient.
Every inefficient act is a failure, and if you spend your life in doing
inefficient acts, your whole life will be a failure.

The more things you do, the worse for you, if all your acts are inefficient ones. On the other hand, every efficient act is a success in itself, and if every act of your life is an efficient one, your whole life MUST be a success. *(See Work Project #2 for a unique way to record this)*

The cause of failure is doing too many things in an inefficient manner, and not doing enough things in an efficient manner. You will see that it is a self-evident proposition that if you do not do any inefficient acts, and if you do a sufficient number of efficient acts, you will become rich. If, now, it is possible for you to make each act an efficient one, you see again that the getting of riches is reduced to an exact science, like mathematics.

The matter turns, then, on the question whether you can make each separate act a success in itself. And this you can certainly do. You can make each act a success, because ALL Power is working with you; and ALL Power cannot fail. Power is at your service; and to make each act efficient, you have only to put power into it. Every action is either strong or weak; and when every one is strong, you are acting in the certain way, which will make you rich. Every act can be made strong and efficient by holding your vision while you are doing it, and putting the whole power of your FAITH and PURPOSE into it.

It is at this point that the people who fail, separate mental power from personal action. They use the power of mind in one place and at one time, and they act in another place and at another time. So their acts are not successful in themselves; too many of them are inefficient. But if ALL Power goes into every act, no matter how commonplace, every act will be a success in itself; and as in the nature of things, every success opens the way to other successes, your progress toward what you want, and the progress of what you want toward you, will increase rapidly.

Remember that successful action is cumulative in its results. Since the desire for more life is inherent in all things, when a person begins to move toward larger life, more things attach themselves, and the influence of desire is multiplied.

Do, every day, all that you can do that day, and do each act in an efficient manner.

In saying that you must hold your vision while you are doing each act, however trivial or commonplace, I do not mean to say that it is necessary at all times to see the vision distinctly to its smallest details. It should be the work of your leisure hours to use your imagination on the details of your vision, and to contemplate them until they are firmly fixed upon memory. If you wish speedy results, spend practically all your spare time in this practice.

By continuous contemplation, you will get the picture of what you want, so firmly fixed upon your mind, and so completely transferred to the mind of Formless Substance, that in your working hours, you only need to mentally refer to it to stimulate your faith and purpose, and cause your best effort to be put forth. Contemplate your picture in your leisure hours until your consciousness is so full of it that you can grasp it instantly. You will become so enthused with its bright promise, that the mere thought of it will call forth the strongest energies of your whole being.

Let us again repeat our syllabus, and by slightly changing the closing statements bring it to the point we have now reached.

There is a thinking stuff from which all things are made, and which, in its original state, permeates, penetrates, and fills the interspaces of the universe.

A thought, in this substance, produces the thing that is imaged by the thought.

51

A person can form things in thought, and, by impressing thought upon formless substance, can cause the thing thought about to be created. In order to do this, you must pass from the competitive to the creative mind; you must form a clear mental picture of the things you want, and do, with faith and purpose, all that can be done each day, doing each separate thing in an efficient manner.

CHAPTER 13- Getting into the Right Business

Success, in any particular business, depends for one thing upon your possessing, in a well-developed state- the skills required for that business.

Without good musical talent, no one can succeed as a musician; without well-developed mechanical skills no one can achieve great success as a mechanic; without business saavy, no one can succeed in business. But to possess in a well-developed state the skills required in your particular vocation does not insure getting rich. There are musicians who have remarkable talent, and remain poor; there are mechanics who have excellent mechanical ability, but who do not get rich; and there are merchants with good skills for dealing with business who nevertheless fail.

The different skills are tools; it is essential to have good tools, but it is also essential that the tools should be used in the right way. One person can take a saw, a screw driver, a good piece of wood, and build a handsome piece of furniture; another person can take the same tools and set to work duplicating it, but his piece will be a mess. They do not know how to use good tools in a successful way.

The various skills of your mind are the tools with which you must work towards your goal of wealth. It will be easier for you to succeed if you get into a business which you are well equipped with mental tools. Generally speaking, you will do best in that business which will use your strongest skills; the one for which you are naturally best suited. But no one should regard his vocation as being irrevocably fixed by the talents with which he was born.

You can get rich in ANY business; if you do not have the right talent, you can develop that talent; it merely means that you will have to make your tools as you go, instead of confining yourself to the use of those with which you were born. It will be EASIER for you to succeed in a vocation for which you already have the talents in a well-developed state; but you CAN succeed in any vocation, because you can develop any rudimentary talent.

You will get rich most easily if you do that for which you are best suited; but you will also get rich if you do what you WANT to do. Doing what you want to do IS life; and there is no real satisfaction in living if we are compelled to forever be doing something we don't like, and can never do what we want to do. And it is certain that you can do what you want to do; the *desire* to do it is proof that you have within you the power which *can* do it.

Desire is a manifestation of power. The desire to play music is the power which can play music, seeking expression and development; the desire to invent is the inventive talent seeking expression and development.

Where there is no power, either developed or undeveloped to do a thing, there is never any desire to do that thing; and where there is strong desire to do a thing, it is certain proof that the power to do it is strong, and only requires to be developed and applied in the right way.

All things being equal, it is best to select the business for which you have the best developed talent; but if you have a strong desire to engage in any particular line of work, you should select that work as the ultimate end at which you aim.

You can do what you want to do, and it's your right and privilege to follow the business or vocation which will be most fun. You are not obliged to do what you do not like to do, and should not do it, except as a means to bring you to the doing of the thing you want to do.

If there are past mistakes whose consequences have placed you in an undesirable business or environment, you may be obliged for some time to do what you do not like to do; but you can make the doing more pleasant by knowing that it's making it possible for you to do what you want to do.

If you feel that you are not in the right vocation, do not act too hastily in trying to get into another one. The best way, generally, to change business or environment is by growth. Do not be afraid to make a sudden and radical change if the opportunity is presented, and you feel after careful consideration that it's the right opportunity; but never take sudden or radical action when you are in doubt as to the wisdom of doing so.

There is never any hurry on the creative plane; and there is no lack of opportunity. When you get out of the competitive mind, you will understand that you never need to act hastily. No one else is going to beat you to the thing you want to do; there is enough for all. If one space is taken, another and a better one will be opened for you a little farther on; there is plenty of time. When you are in doubt, wait. Fall back on the contemplation of your vision, and increase your faith and purpose; and by all means, in times of doubt and indecision, cultivate gratitude.

A day or two spent in contemplating the vision of what you want, and in earnest thanksgiving that you are getting it, will bring your mind into such close relationship with the Supreme that you will make no mistake when you do act. There is a mind, which knows all there is to know; and you can come into close unity with this mind by faith and the purpose to advance in life, if you have deep gratitude.

54

Mistakes come from acting hastily, or from acting in fear or doubt, or in forgetfulness of the right motive, which is more life to all, and less to none. As you go on in the certain way, opportunities will come to you in increasing number; and you will need to be very steady in your faith and purpose, and to keep in close touch with the All Mind by reverent gratitude.

Do all that you can do in a perfect manner every day, but do it without haste, worry, or fear. Go as fast as you can, but never hurry. Remember that in the moment you begin to hurry, you cease to be a creator and become a competitor; you drop back upon the old plane again. Whenever you find yourself hurrying, stop; fix your attention on the mental image of the thing you want, and begin to give thanks that you are getting it. The exercise of GRATITUDE will never fail to strengthen your faith and renew your purpose.

CHAPTER 14- The Impression of Increase

Whether you change your vocation or not, your actions for the present must be those pertaining to the business in which you are now engaged. You can get into the business you want by making constructive use of the business you are already established in; by doing your daily work in a certain way. And in so far as your business consists in dealing with other people, whether personally, or by phone or e-mail, the key-thought of all your efforts must be to convey to their minds the impression of increase.

Increase is what all men and women are seeking; it is the urge of the Formless Intelligence within them, seeking fuller expression. The desire for increase is inherent in all nature; it is the fundamental impulse of the Universe. All human activities are based on the desire for increase; people are seeking better food, better clothes, better shelter, more luxury, more beauty, more knowledge, more pleasure- increase in something, more life!

Every living thing is under this necessity for continuous advancement; where increase of life ceases, dissolution and death set in at once.

Man instinctively knows this, and hence he is forever seeking more. This law of perpetual increase is set forth by Jesus in the parable of the talents; only those who gain more retain any; from him who hath not, shall be taken away, even that which he hath.

The normal desire for increased wealth is not an evil or a reprehensible thing; it is simply the desire for more abundant life; it is aspiration. And because it is the deepest instinct of their natures, all men and women are attracted to the person who can give them more of the means of life.

In following the certain way as described in the foregoing pages, you are getting continuous increase for yourself, and you are giving it to all with whom you deal. You are a creative center, from which increase is given off to all.

Be sure of this, and convey assurance of the fact to every man, woman, and child with whom you come in contact. No matter how small the transaction, even if it's only selling an ice cream cone to a child, put into it the thought of increase, and make sure that the customer is impressed with the thought. Convey the impression of advancement with everything you do, so that all people shall receive the impression that you are an Advancing Person, and that you advance all who deal with you. Even to the people whom you meet in a social way, without any thought of business, and to whom you do not try to sell anything, give the thought of increase. You can convey this impression by holding the unshakable faith that you, yourself, are in the way of increase; and by letting this faith inspire, fill, and permeate every action. Do everything that you do in the firm conviction that you are an advancing personality, and that you are giving advancement to everybody.

Feel that you are getting rich, and that in doing so you are making others rich, and conferring benefits on all. Do not boast or brag about your success, or talk about it unnecessarily; true faith is never boastful. Wherever you find a boastful person, you find one who is secretly doubtful and afraid. Simply feel the faith, and let it work out in every transaction; let every act and tone and look express the quiet assurance that you are getting rich; that you already are rich. Words will not be necessary to communicate this feeling to others; they will feel the sense of increase when in your presence, and will be attracted to you.

You must so impress others, that they will feel that in associating with you, they will get increase for themselves. See that you give them a use value greater than the cash value you are taking from them. Take an honest pride in doing this, and let everybody know it; and you will have no lack of customers. People will go where they are given increase; and the Supreme, which desires increase in all, and which knows all, will move toward you people who have never heard of you. Your business will increase rapidly, and you will be surprised at the unexpected benefits which will come to you. You will be able, from day to day, to make larger combinations, secure greater advantages, and to go on into a more congenial vocation if you desire to do so.

But doing all this, you must never lose sight of your vision of what you want, or your faith and purpose to get what you want.

Let me here give you another word of caution in regard to motives. Beware of the insidious temptation to seek power over other people. Nothing is so pleasant to the unformed or partially developed mind as the exercise of power over others. *The desire to rule for selfish gratification has been the curse of the world.* For countless ages kings and lords have drenched the earth with blood in their battles to extend their dominions; this not to seek more life for all, but to get more power for themselves.

Today, the main motive in the business and industrial world is the same; men marshal their armies of dollars, and lay waste the lives and hearts of millions in the same mad scramble for power over others. Corporate kings, like political kings, are inspired by the lust for power.

Look out for the temptation to seek authority, to become a "master", to be considered as one who is above the common herd, to impress others by conspicuous consumption, and so on. The mind that seeks for mastery over others is the competitive mind; and the competitive mind is not the creative one. In order to master your environment and your destiny, it is not at all necessary that you should rule over your fellow men andwomen, and indeed, when you fall into the world's struggle for the high places, you begin to be conquered by fate and environment, and your getting rich becomes a matter of chance and speculation.

Beware of the competitive mind; say to yourself, "What I want for myself, I want for everybody."

CHAPTER 15- The Advancing Person

What I have said in the last chapter applies as well to the professional person and the employee, as well as the merchant. No matter whether you are a physician, a teacher, or a clergyman, if you can give increase of life to others, and make them sensible of the fact, they will be attracted to you, and you will get rich. What is true of the teacher, preacher, and physician is true of the lawyer, dentist, real estate agent, insurance agent.... of everybody. The combined mental and personal action I have described is infallible; it cannot fail. Every man and woman who follows these instructions steadily, perseveringly, and to the letter, will get rich. The law of the Increase of Life is as mathematically certain in its operation as the law of gravity.

The employee will find this as true in their case as of any independent or professional person. Don't feel you have no chance to get rich because you are working where there is no visible opportunity, where wages are low and the cost of living high. Form your clear mental vision of what you want, and begin to act with faith and purpose. Do all the work you can do, every day, and do each piece of work in a perfectly successful manner; put the power of success, and the purpose to get rich, into everything that you do.

But do not do this merely with the idea of gaining favor with your employer, in the hope that he, or those above you, will see your good work and advance you; it is not likely that they will do so. The person who is merely a "good employee", filling their place to the very best of their ability, and satisfied with that, is valuable to their employer; and it is not to the employer's interest to promote them; he or she is worth more exactly where they are!

To secure advancement, something more is necessary than to be too large for your place. The person who is certain to advance is the one who is too big for their place, and who has a clear concept of what they want to be; who knows that they can become, what they want to be, and who is determined to BE what they want to be.

Do not try to more than fill your present place with a view to pleasing your employer; do it with the idea of advancing yourself. Hold the faith and purpose of increase during work hours, after work hours, and before work hours. Hold it in such a way that every person who comes in contact with you, whether foreman, fellow employee, or social acquaintance, will feel the power of purpose radiating from you; so that every one will get the sense of advancement and increase from you. People will be attracted to you, and if there is no possibility for advancement in your present job, you will very soon see an opportunity to take another job.

There is a Power, which never fails to present opportunity to the Advancing Person who is moving in obedience to the law. Intelligent Substance cannot help helping you, if you act in a certain way; It must do so in order to help Itself.

There is nothing in your circumstances or in the industrial situation that can keep you down. If you cannot get rich working for a corporation, you can get rich on a ten-acre farm; and if you begin to move in the certain way, you will certainly escape from the "clutches" of the corporate world, and get on to the farm or wherever else you wish to be. If a few thousand of its employees would enter upon this course, the corporations would soon be in a bad situation; they would have to give their employees more opportunity, or go out of business. Nobody has to work for a corporation; the corporations can keep people in so called hopeless conditions only so long as there are people who are too ignorant to know the principles in this book, or too intellectually lazy to practice it.

Begin this way of thinking and acting, and your faith and purpose will make you quick to see any opportunity to better your condition. Such opportunities will speedily come, for the Supreme, working in All, and working for you, will bring them to you.

Do not wait for an opportunity to be all that you want to be; when an opportunity to be more than you are now is presented, and you feel impelled toward it, take it. It will be the first step toward a greater opportunity. There is no such thing possible in this universe as a lack of opportunities for the person who is living the advancing life.

It is inherent in the constitution of the cosmos that all things shall be for you, and work together for your good; and you must certainly get rich if you act and think in a certain way. So let wage-earning men and women study this book with great care, and enter with confidence upon the course of action it prescribes; it will not fail.

CHAPTER 16- Some Cautions, and Concluding Observations

Many people will scoff at the idea that there is an exact quantum science to getting rich; holding the impression that the supply of wealth is limited, they will insist that social and governmental institutions must be changed before any considerable number of people can acquire a decent income. But this is not true. It is true that existing governments keep the masses in poverty, but this is because the masses do not think and act in a certain way.

If the masses begin to move forward as suggested in this book, neither governments nor corporations can stop them; all systems must be modified to accommodate the forward movement. If the people have the Advancing Mind, have the Faith that they can become rich, and move forward with the fixed purpose to become rich, nothing can possibly keep them in poverty.

Individuals may enter upon the course of action prescribed in this book at any time, and under any government, and make themselves rich; and when any considerable number of individuals do so under any government, they will cause the system to be so modified as to open the way for others.

The more men who get rich on the competitive plane, the worse for others; the more who get rich on the creative plane, the better for others.

The economic salvation of the masses can only be accomplished by getting a large number of people to practice the quantum scientific method set down in this book, and become rich. These will show others the way, and inspire them with a desire for real life, with the faith that it can be attained, and with the purpose to attain it.

For the present, however, it is enough to know that neither the government under which you live, nor the capitalistic or competitive system of industry can keep you from getting rich. When you enter upon the creative plane of thought, you will rise above all these things and become a citizen of another kingdom.

But remember, your thought must be held upon the creative plane; you are never for an instant to believe the supply is limited, or act on the moral level of competition. Whenever you do fall into old ways of thought, correct yourself instantly; for when you are in the competitive mind, you have lost the cooperation of the Mind of the Whole.

Do not spend any time in planning as to how you will meet possible emergencies in the future, except as the necessary policies may affect your actions today. You are concerned with doing today's work in a perfectly successful manner, and not with emergencies which may arise tomorrow; you can deal with them as they come.

Do not concern yourself with questions as to how you will surmount obstacles, which may loom on your horizon, unless you can see plainly that your course must be altered today in order to avoid them.
No matter how big an obstruction may appear at a distance, you will find that if you go on in a certain way, it will disappear as you approach it, or that a way over, through, or around it will appear. Give no anxious thought to possible disasters, obstacles, pains, or unfavorable circumstances; it is time enough to meet such things when they present themselves in the immediate present, and you will find that every difficulty carries with it the wherewithal for its overcoming.

Guard your speech. Never speak of yourself, your affairs, or of anything else in a discouraged or discouraging way. Never admit the possibility of failure, or speak in a way that infers failure as a possibility.

62

Never speak of the times as being hard, or of business conditions being doubtful. Times may be hard, and business doubtful, for those who are on the competitive plane, but they can never be so for you; you can create what you want, and you are above fear. When others are having hard times and poor business, you will find your greatest opportunities.

Train yourself to think of and to look upon the world as a something which is Becoming, which is growing; and to regard seeming evil as being only that which is undeveloped. Always speak in terms of advancement; to do otherwise is to deny your faith, and to deny your faith is to lose it.

Never allow yourself to feel disappointed. You may expect to have a certain thing at a certain time, and not get it; and this will appear like failure. But if you hold to your faith, you will find that the failure is only apparent. Go on in the certain way, and if you do not receive that thing, you will receive something so much better, that you will see that the seeming failure was really a great success!

A student of this quantum science had set their mind on making a certain business deal, which seemed at the time very desirable, and they worked for weeks to make it happen. When the crucial time came, the thing failed in a perfectly inexplicable way; it was as if some unseen force had been working secretly against them. The student was not disappointed; on the contrary, they thanked God that the desire had been overruled, and went steadily on with a grateful mind. In a few weeks, an opportunity so much better came their way, that they would not have made the first deal on any account; and they saw that a Mind which knew more than they knew had prevented them from losing the greater good by entangling themselves with the lesser.

That is the way every seeming failure will work out for you, if you keep your faith, hold to your purpose, have gratitude, and do, every day, all that can be done that day, doing each separate act in a successful manner. *When you make a failure, it is because you have not asked for enough; keep on, and something larger will certainly come to you.* Remember this- you will not fail because you lack the necessary talent to do what you wish to do. If you go on as directed, you will develop all the talent necessary to the doing of your chosen work.

It is not within the scope of this book to deal with the science of cultivating talent; but it is as certain and simple as the process of getting rich. However, do not hesitate or waver for fear that when you come to any certain place you will fail for lack of ability; keep right on, and when you come to that place, the ability will be there. The same source of ability which enabled the untaught Lincoln to do the greatest work as President is open to you; you may draw upon all the mind there is, for wisdom to use in meeting the responsibilities which are laid upon you. Go on in full faith.

Study this book. Make it your constant companion until you have mastered all the ideas contained in it. While you are getting firmly established in this faith, you will do well to stay away from places where conflicting ideas are advanced. Do not read pessimistic or conflicting literature, or get into arguments on the matter. Spend most of your leisure time contemplating your vision, and in cultivating gratitude, and in reading this book. It contains all you need to know; and you will find all the essentials summed up in the following chapter.

CHAPTER 17- Summary

There is a thinking stuff from which all things are made, and which, in its original state, permeates, penetrates, and fills the interspaces of the universe.

A thought in this substance produces the thing that is imaged by the thought. A person can form things in thought, and by impressing thought upon formless substance, can cause the thing thought about to be created.

In order to do this, you must pass from the competitive to the creative mind; otherwise you cannot be in harmony with the Formless Intelligence, which is always creative and never competitive in spirit.

A person may come into full harmony with the Formless Substance by entertaining a lively and sincere gratitude for the blessings it bestows. Gratitude unifies the mind with the intelligence of Substance, so that a person's thoughts are received by the Formless. You can remain upon the creative plane only by uniting yourself with the Formless Intelligence, through a deep and continuous feeling of gratitude.

You must form a clear and definite mental image of the things you wishes to have, to do, or to become; and you must hold this mental image in your thoughts, while being deeply grateful to the Supreme that all your desires are granted to you. The person who wishes to get rich must spend their leisure hours contemplating their Vision, and in earnest thanksgiving that the reality is being given to them. Too much stress cannot be laid on the importance of frequent contemplation of the mental image, coupled with unwavering faith and devout gratitude. This is the process by which the impression is given to the Formless, and the creative forces set in motion.

The creative energy works through the established channels of natural growth, and of the industrial and social order. All that is included in the mental image will surely be brought to the person who follows the instructions given above, and whose faith does not waver. What they want will come to them through the ways of established trade and commerce.

In order to receive their own when it comes, a person must be active; and this activity can only consist in more than filling their present place. They must keep in mind the Purpose to get rich through the realization of their mental image. And they must do, every day, all that can be done that day, taking care to do each act in a successful manner. They must give to everyone a use value in excess of the cash value they receive, so that each transaction makes for more life; and they must so hold the Advancing Thought that the impression of increase will be communicated to all they come in contact with.

The men and women who practice the foregoing instructions will certainly get rich; and the riches they receive will be in exact proportion to the definiteness of their vision, the fixity of their purpose, the steadiness of their faith, and the depth of their gratitude.

APPENDIX A- Brain Wave States

(You can purchase Dr. Jane Ma'ati Smith's "Science of Getting Rich" binaural beat self hypnosis and subliminal audio program from her website www.subliminalselfhypnosis.com or at Amazon.com to compliment this book)

Scientists have discovered that our brains operate in four levels of frequency- beta, alpha, theta and delta. Each level of frequency is measured in cycles per second, or hertz- hz.

Beta has the highest frequency, between 13 and 40 cycles per second. This is associated with our normal waking state. Beta helps in logical thinking, analysis and active attention. Stress can throw the frequency to the higher ranges of beta.

Alpha operates between 8 and 13 cycles per second. This occurs during daydreaming, fantasizing and creative visualization. This is often associated with a deeply relaxed state, and with a light trance or meditation.

Theta operates between 4 and 8 cycles per second. Theta is associated with intuition, and allows us to access our subconscious. It is activated during dream sleep and deep meditational states. Theta is also associated with creative thinking, and allows us to tap into our inner genius.

Delta has the lowest frequency between 0.5 and 4 cycles per second. Delta is produced during deep sleep.

The "Science of Getting Rich" self hypnosis audio begins at a Beta frequency of 16 hz, and gradually ramps down to a frequency of 7.8 (the "Earth Resonance" or Shumman Frequency). This is a low Alpha/high Theta state, very good for accessing the subconscious (and in my opinion, good for putting you into the frequency for creating.... That of Mother Earth). It also incorporates a Solfeggio frequency of 417 Hz as the balance of the binaural beat- this frequency is reputed to "shake loose" old thought patterns and habits from the cells of your brain and body, so that you can more easily bring about change; exactly your goal with getting rich!

To best use this audio, it is suggested that you consciously take the time to relax *before* you start- the closer you brain already is to the beginning frequency of 16 hz, the deeper you will be able to go. If you are upset, stressed out, have racing thoughts, (in the higher Beta ranges, maybe 25- 40 hz) the self hypnosis program will still be very a very calming experience, but you will probably not reach the low point of 7.8 hz. The binaural beat can only do so much, so it's good to try and meet it half way! So before you begin, try and clear your mind, and relax.

What Are Binaural Beats?

If two different tones are played into each ear, the brain attempts to find a balance- for example, if the frequency of sound in your left ear is 420Hz, and the frequency you're hearing in your right ear is 430Hz, your brain will process a binaural beat of about 10Hz. These beats are not actually heard, since they are well below the natural range of hearing, but you can often "hear" a sort of "humming" inside your head as the binaural beat.

It's been discovered that these beats can be used to elicit responses in the brain; the brain becomes "entrained", which means it starts to resonate at the same frequency as the binaural beat. When this happens, it can change the brain wave patterns in your brain temporarily. This has been shown to have a huge effect- it's been shown that these binaural beats are highly effective at inducing meditative and hypnotic states. This is a great breakthrough for anyone wants to meditate, but didn't have the time or teacher to learn how. This type of meditation is also more effective than usual meditation because of the binaural beats. It can reduce your stress levels, the amount of sleep you need, and it can increase such things as intelligence, intuition and creativity.

Just listening to a binaural beat will not necessarily cause a state of altered consciousness- it works best if you help the beat along, by reducing distractions, consciously relaxing, and having a desire let go, and to be in that state of consciousness.

Again, using binaural beats can:

*Safely and easily take you to a state of deep meditation.

*Stimulate the creation of new neural pathways between the right and left hemispheres of your brain, leading you to a high performance state called whole brain functioning.

*Dramatically improves your learning ability, memory, intuition, creativity, your ability to focus, concentrate and think more clearly.

*Create quantum leaps in your personal self awareness

*Significantly lower your stress levels.

*Create improvements in your mental and emotional health, even areas that have stubbornly resisted change with other approaches.

*Dramatically increase your production of vital brain chemicals related to your longevity, well-being, and quality of life.

What Are Solfeggio Frequencies?

These original sound frequencies were used in Ancient Gregorian Chants, such as the great hymn to St. John the Baptist. The chants and their special tones were believed to impart tremendous spiritual blessings when sung in harmony during religious masses.

The Six Solfeggio Frequencies include:

UT – 396 Hz – Liberating Guilt and Fear
RE – 417 Hz – Undoing Situations and Facilitating Change
MI – 528 Hz – Transformation and Miracles (DNA Repair)
FA – 639 Hz – Connecting/Relationships
SOL – 741 Hz – Awakening Intuition
LA – 852 Hz – Returning to Spiritual Order

These frequencies are reputed to have many psycho-spiritual and physical healing benefits- the third note, frequency 528, relates to the note MI on the Western musical scale, and derives from the phrase "MI-ra gestorum", which in Latin means "miracle." Amazingly, this is the exact frequency used by genetic biochemists to repair broken DNA – the genetic blueprint upon which life is based!

For the "Science of Getting Rich" program, I have chosen a frequency of 417 hz- "Undoing situations, and facilitating change". This seems like just the frequency needed to "undo" your current "poverty consciousness" and facilitate your change into "prosperity consciousness!"

Subliminal Programs

A subliminal program is a highly focused message embedded into something such as music; subliminals are designed to avoid the critical, doubting, self sabotaging nature of your own thoughts. These accelerated subliminal messages are able to sidestep the critical conscious mind, and it is assumed they are captured, comprehended and implemented readily by the subconscious mind.

Although science has not been able to definitively prove or disprove the validity of subliminal suggestion, believers in the power of subliminal suggestion claim the ability to circumvent the critical nature of the conscious mind is extremely powerful, and therefore subliminal suggestions are potentially more effective than ordinary suggestions. The subliminal messages embedded in the "Get Rich" program are identical to those in the "Science of Getting Rich" self hypnosis program, minus the hypnotic induction. If you have experienced your conscious mind resisting and negating the ideas and habits that would benefit you, if you have a tendency towards self sabotage and resistance, subliminal programming may be for you!

The "music" I have created for the subliminal component of the "Science of Getting Rich" program is not really music per se'.... rather, it is a soothing composition of Solfeggio frequencies, flowing water, Tibetan bells and crystal bowls, combined with a deep Beta/ light Alpha binaural beat to put you into a light and relaxing trance. In my experience, subliminals work best when combined with self hypnosis- the subliminal suggestions are the same as the suggestions in the hypnosis program.

Some Tips on Deepening Your Experience

1. Before you put on your headphones, relax. Scan your body for tension, and relax, release it.
2. By simulating some of the physical effects of hypnosis, you can trigger your body to follow- one easy way to do this is to allow your eyes to roll up- this will trigger your brain to fall into an Alpha state. Also, allow your eyelids to relax completely.
3. Focus on the binaural beats- center your attention into the center of your head, about an inch or two behind the point between your eyebrows.
4. Breathe deeply through your abdomen, not your chest. Abdominal breathing induces relaxation. Keep your breathe deep and even, and relax with each exhale.
5. Let your jaw drop. Keep your eyes closed. And allow it to work!

(You can purchase Dr. Jane Ma'ati Smith's "Science of Getting Rich" binaural beat self hypnosis and subliminal audio program from her website www.subliminalselfhypnosis.com or at Amazon.com to compliment this book)

APPENIDX B- About Energy and Meditations to Improve Focus

Physics is a science that studies the interactions between matter and energy; the prefix "meta" indicates that which goes beyond or transcends- thus, "metaphysics" is the esoteric study of the interaction between energy and matter. It is the very basis of the art and the use of energy to effect the material world.

The physical, material world is made up of atoms and molecules, held together with energy. The nonphysical world of thoughts, emotions and spirit is made of pure energy- it is, in fact, part of a web of energy that holds our perceived reality together. It seems logical then, that if your spirit, thoughts and emotions are part of the web of energy that forms the cohesiveness of reality, that it must then have some effect on it. It does- our thoughts and emotions form our individual and collective reality, through the medium of spiritual energy. The trick is, using this energy to create the reality you want!

The first thing you must understand is this- "As Below, So Above". This means that the reality you create in your outer world is a reflection of your inner world, both conscious and unconscious. Attempting to create with an underlying energy of turmoil, heart break, ego or anger will ultimately bring only more of the same, to not only you, but to those around you. The substance of the Universe is composed of energy; a thought, firmly pressed into this 'substance', with the power of desire and the energy of emotion to feed it, will sprout and grow, like a seed.

All religions have certain spiritual 'Laws', designed to aid their followers in leading more fulfilling lives. We, as individuals, may or may not agree with the 'Laws' of particular religions, but the root of this tradition is important; the world we live in is comprised of energy (to the religious, God), and this energy responds to our thoughts, our actions, and our emotions, thus creating our individual and common reality.

The Basic Laws of Universal Energy

#1- The energy of the Universe responds to our thoughts, both conscious and unconscious, to create our reality. Thus, the first step to creating the reality we want is to align the thoughts of our conscious and unconscious minds with the vision of our desire. Our unconscious mind is not as "unconscious" and hard to access as we'd like to believe- the running dialog we carry on with ourselves, and the sometimes disturbing and intrusive thoughts we push away is our unconscious mind speaking to us, and making its feelings and beliefs known to us. Acknowledge and accept these thoughts, and if they are not aligned with the reality you want to create, don't fight them; instead simply acknowledge them and lovingly release them, allowing the vision you want to grow and take hold.

#2- This Universal energy is *creative*, not *competitive*. The purpose of this energy is to ultimately *create more life*. In order to align yourself with this energy, you must also pass from the competitive to the creative, creating more life for all. No one has to lose in order for you to win; work your magic and live your life so that all will win! Give more than you receive, knowing in your heart the Universal energy will always create more for all.

#3- The Universal energy resonates with the frequency of *Love and Gratitude*. Resonating with the frequency of love and gratitude aligns you with the frequency of the Universal energy, keeping you within the realm of the creative mind. Nurture the seeds you plant within the Creative Mind with love and gratitude, and the Universal energy will grow your vision.

#4- It's ironic, *but the desires you focus most intensely on will often be the most difficult to manifest.* This is because mental and emotional *obsessions* come from a place of *'want'*, and the Universe will respond to the deepest, most underlying emotions powering your desire. *Want* and *need* have a tendency to keep your dreams just out of reach, like the proverbial 'brass ring' on a Merry Go Round. Feel that you *have*, not that you *want*, and nurture a deep sense of gratitude to the Powers that Be for the continual, unfolding manifestation of your dream. Letting go of mental and emotional obsessions will free your spirit to create on many levels!

#5- The Universal Mind works to create through the everyday channels of reality (which is really the energetic 'construct' created by everyone's combined thoughts, emotions, and energy). Open the channels of Universal energy to flow in your direction by actively working within everyday reality to manifest your dreams. It's all about finding the energetic 'flow'. The flow of the Universe is known as "synchronicity".

What is synchronicity?

"Synchronicity" is a term coined by the great psychologist C.G. Jung for "meaningful coincidence", events that seemingly have no causal relationship, but are in fact related on a higher plane of meaning. Have you ever thought of someone, only to run into that person later in the day? Or perhaps you narrowly avoided an accident, by turning the corner at just the right time? Synchronicity happens constantly, but most of us only notice the most obvious instances. Synchronicity is often preceded by deep emotional or mental activity, or, often the mind has been seemingly "distracted" in a state of "day dreaming", and your automatic, unthinking actions led you down the "right path".

Nothing is really a coincidence, and the trail of synchronicity can lead you to meet the right people, at the right place, at the right time, which is really very magic! How can this be done?

#1- Pay attention to what is going on around you, *without analyzing or judging!* Our "inner critic" often dismisses synchronicity, because it doesn't seem logical, it's unexpected, or the person or place presented doesn't meet your own preconceived expectations.

#2- Learn to know the difference between premonition and wishful thinking. Is your urge to go to a certain place motivated by preconceived

74

desires or obsessions- "my ex often goes to that park, I think I'll go to the park" (with the secret hope you'll *"accidentally"* run into him?) Real synchronicity would be the park keeps popping into your mind, for no apparent reason or ulterior motives. You go, and maybe you meet no one, but it was nice to get outside, and you feel renewed. Or, maybe you meet an old coworker from an old job, someone you hadn't even thought of, who gives you a lead for a new job.... which leads you to meet new people, which leads you to meet your soul mate, months later!

#3- Understand that the trip is half the fun! The results of your "creative" workings most likely will not land neatly in your lap. What is most likely to happen is that the *intent* you put into your creating will subtly change the energetic flow around you- so the message is, go with the flow! Recognize and follow the trail of synchronicity that has magically opened before you.

How to distinguish synchronicity and premonition from wishful thinking

Wishful thinking is generally accompanied by a feeling of anxiety, the thoughts keep popping into your head, but there is an intrusive quality to it. You get the feeling you should go somewhere or do something, but are mentally planning on some level what you would like to happen, relating to an obsession. You want something specific to happen, and are semi-consciously scanning for an opening.

Synchronicity is generally accompanied by a sense of calm, of mindlessness, a feeling that you should follow your feelings, but really don't know why. The path is laid out by honest desires, that which will lead you to develop your true self. We are all born into this life with certain innate talents, with certain spiritual goals, and the path to real, beneficial creation relies on self knowledge, and the ability to let go of false desires and obsessions. Synchronicity might lead us to people and places we've never even dreamed of, for reasons we can't even imagine. But finding that path is the key to leading a truly magical life!

MEDITATION

Before I get into the meditations, let me define the word **Chakra-** it is a Sanskrit (Hindu) word meaning "spinning wheel of energy". These energy centers within our bodies receive and transmit energy, and each is situated at a major endocrine gland, and nerve bundle within the physical body, called a plexus. Each chakra is connected and associated with a different part of the body. There are seven chakras. Understanding and using your chakras can promote physical, emotional and spiritual healing, and can lend energy to your manifesting.

A tip about the "Third Eye" Chakra..... people often assume the "brow chakra" or "Third Eye" is in the *center of the forehead, right between the eyes*. This IS NOT SO. This chakra is actually *in the center of the brain.* Please try this experiment- pull your "attention" away from your forehead, back into the center of your brain... does your mind quiet? Is there less 'mind chatter'? You see, when you mentally and energetically 'reach out' to meet a person or a situation, you are becoming 'uncentered' and stimulating 'mind chatter'. Just stay right in the *center of your head,* and allow the people and situations *to come to you.* There is nothing wrong with this- in fact, it more easily allows them to stay "centered", and they will be easier to deal with!

Another chakra centering technique is to remain balanced at the heart chakra- the ancient Egyptians, one of the most amazingly creative, wealthy and advanced civilizations of the ancient world, actually believed the heart was the center of *thought.* In other words, they believed the *brain was in the heart, not the head!* What this tells me is, the Egyptians remained "centered" at their heart chakra, and this is where they created from.

The top three chakras- the crown, third eye and throat- are the seat of your masculine energy. They are responsible for critical and analytical thought, logic and reason.

The lower three chakras- the root, navel and solar plexus- are the seat of your feminine energy. They are responsible for your emotional reactions and memories, your creativity, and your capacity for childlike wonder and delight.

The heart chakra is where the male and female energies meet- it is the most potent place from which to imagine and visualize your desires. Staying centered in the heart will help you avoid the pointless mind chatter of the masculine, and the anxious worry of the feminine; stay focused on your heart's desire for the best results!

Controlling the flow of your own energy is not only the key to success, but to your happiness and health. How do you do this? Through practicing the art of meditation.

Five Pointed Star Meditation

Find a quiet place and time, where you can have at least fifteen minutes of peace and quiet. Lie down, with your arms and legs gently spread apart- comfortably, and not too wide. Make sure your hands are facing palms up.

Feel yourself sinking into the floor, just melting and glowing, feeling very heavy. Locate the chakras in your hands and feet- your hand chakras are in the center of your palms, and your feet chakras are in the center of the arch of your feet. Open these chakras up, and feel energy flowing through them, and up your arms and legs. Let the energy flow up to your heart chakra- combine the energy from your arms and legs in your heart center. From the heart center, let the energy flow freely upwards, through the center of your head, and out the crown charkra. Let this energy fountain out through your crown, flowing out into your aura. Feel your aura glowing big and bright, like a star.

Keep glowing until you feel your energy field is whole and complete. Gently relax the flow of energy, until you feel solid, and back to the 'real world'. Your mind should now be free of clutter, and your body should feel energized!

Sacred Tree Meditation

The Buddha found Enlightenment while meditating under a Bo tree. This quick and easy meditation may not free you from the Cycles of Rebirth or the Wheel of Karma, but it might just free you from the psychic stress and tensions of your day to day life, thus enabling you to focus more clearly on your true purpose.

Find a quiet place and time, take off your shoes, close your eyes, and stand with your hands hanging heavily at your side. Imagine yourself surrounded by a warm, white light, and breathe this energy in, deeply and slowly.

Feel your feet on the floor, and imagine growing roots- let these roots grow way down deep, right to the center of the Earth. As these roots ground you and connect you to our Mother Earth, release all the psychic negativity of your day- release all the people, the problems, all the responsibilities back to the Earth. Breathe deeply, and feel all the energy that's been keeping you from feeling grounded and centered drain out, and into the core of the Earth.

Now, imagine your roots absorbing the nourishment Mother Earth has to offer- feel this warm, powerful energy from the Earth's core rise up through your roots, through your feet, your legs, your hips, your torso. When you fell the energy reach your shoulders, let your tree grow branches. Reach these branches up into the Universe, far out into the Cosmos. Feel the psychic energy of the Universe flowing through your branches, through your head, and down through your trunk. Allow this Cosmic clairvoyant energy to flow right down through your roots, into the Earth. Feel the Earth energy rising up, the Cosmic flowing down. You are now grounded to the Earth, and in tune with the Cosmos.

When you are ready, call back all the psychic energy you've lost and left behind through out the day, and gather it up into a hot, glowing golden sun above your head. Let this gold sun of your own psychic energy flow through your head, down your arms, filling up your entire body, right down to your feet. If you want, make another gold sun to shine down and nourish your "tree". When you are ready, open your eyes, stretch, and feel refreshed!

Zhang Fu Theory, Chakras, "Cellular Memory" and An Advanced Meditation

Have you ever considered the idea that you might not be storing all of your memories *in your head?* Many people believe that we also store our memories *in our bodies, especially the emotionally charged memories,* and that this can contribute or even cause physical illness and disease.

Have you ever considered that maybe, some of your persistent health complaints might be related to some of your other life difficulties? Or visa versa? One good book I can recommend on that subject is, "You Can Heal Your Life" by Louise Hay. Basically, the idea is, when we hold on to negative emotions, these are based in certain parts of the body, and will eventually manifest as a dis-ease. Also, there are certain theories about what organs go with what types of thoughts and emotions. The "Get Rich" audio programs are set at a Solfeggio frequency of 417 hz, which relates most closely with the vibration of the 2nd chakra, which is based in your abdomen. So could it be, (not to be crude, but....) that you are financially constipated? Or perhaps suffering from financial diarrhea? *This is just an example. Your particular "cellular memory" relating to your finances could be stored anywhere!*

In traditional Chinese medicine, there is something known as "Zhang Fu theory". The theory states there are five Zhang (solid) organs and five Fu (hollow) organs. Each Zhang organ has a function, an element, an associated Fu organ, an associated emotion, spirit, etc.

Zhang-fu relationships, Emotions, Spirits and Spirit Acupressure points

Element	Fire	Earth	Metal/Air	Water	Wood
Zhang Organ	heart	spleen	lungs	kidneys	liver
Related Fu Organ	Small intestine	stomach	Large Intestine	bladder	gall bladder
Emotion	Joy	Pensiveness	Grief	Fear	Anger
Spirit	Cosmic Soul	Intellect	Corporeal Soul	Will	Ethereal Soul
Acupressure or acupuncture point	*Shentang-* Spirit Hall- BL44 **Location:** ½ way between your armpit and spine on the left side of your back	*Yishe-*Idea Abode- BL49 **Location:** ½ way between your waist and spine on the left side of your back	*Pohu-* BL42 **Location:** ½ way between your shoulder/ upper arm and spine on the left side of your back	*Zhishi-*Will Chamber- BL52 **Location:** 2" out from 2nd lumbar vertebrae, right above butt muscle on left side	*Hunmen-* Soul Gate- BL47 **Location:** 2" out from 9th thoracic vertebrae, middle back on left side

(Maybe next time you get a massage, try pressing these points, to see if anything can be released!)

The seven chakras also have related organs and illnesses-

The First Chakra:
Located at the base of the spine, color is red.
Related organs- The spinal column, bones, feet, and the immune system.
Energy- physical safety, security, your ability to provide for life's necessities, courage and inner strength.
Physical disorders- Lower back pain, sciatica, varicose veins, rectal problems, depression, immune disorders.

Second Chakra:
Located about three fingers below the navel. Color is orange.
Related organs- Sexual organs, large intestine, pelvis, appendix, bladder, hips.
Energy- Blame, guilt, money, sex, power and control, creativity, joy, sociability.
Physical disorders- Lower back pain, reproductive problems, urinary problems, constipation and/or diarrhea, gas and bloating.

Third Chakra:
Located just below the center of the rib cage. Color is yellow.
Related organs- Abdomen, small intestine, liver, gallbladder, kidney and pancreas, adrenal glands, spleen.
Energy- Issues of trust, feelings of fear and intimidation, self-esteem, self-respect, caring for ones self and others, decisions, sensitivity to criticism, sense of honor.
Physical disorders- Arthritis, ulcers, diabetes, indigestion, eating disorders, liver.

Fourth Chakra:

Located in the center of the chest. Color is green.

Related organs- Heart and circulatory system, lungs, shoulders and arms, ribs, breasts, diaphragm, thymus gland.

Energy- Love and hate, resentment, bitterness, grief, anger, self-centeredness, loneliness, commitment, forgiveness, compassion, hope and trust.

Physical disorders- Heart disease, asthma, allergies, bronchial conditions, upper back, shoulder, breast cancers.

Fifth Chakra:

Located in the center of the throat. Color is light blue.

Related organs- Throat, thyroid, mouth, teeth, gums, esophagus.

Energy- Sense of choice and personal expression, strength of will, following your dream, using your personal power to create, addictions, judgment, criticism, faith and knowledge, ability to make decisions.

Physical disorders- sore throat, raspy voice, mouth ulcers, gum disease, TMJ, swollen glands, thyroid problems.

Sixth Chakra:

Located between and just above the center of the eyebrows, in the middle of your head. Color is indigo.

Related organs- The brain, nervous system, eyes, ears, nose, pineal gland, and pituitary gland.

Energy- Self evaluation, truth, intellect, sense of adequacy, openness to new ideas, your ability to learn from experience, emotional intelligence, connection to intuition.

Physical disorders- Brain disorders, neurological disorders, blindness, deafness, learning disabilities, seizures.

Seventh Chakra:
Located at the crown on the head. Color is violet.

Related organs- Muscular system, skeletal system, skin.

Energy- Ability to trust in the process of life, personal values, ethics, courage, humanitarianism, faith, inspiration, spirituality and devotion.

Physical Disorders- Energetic disorders, depression, chronic fatigue, extreme sensitivity to light or sound.

OK, so where am I going with this? Just demonstrating that this is an old and valid theory, and to maybe give you some food for thought. What are your predominant, negative emotions? Where do your health problems manifest? And might any of this relate in any way to the reasons why you have problems making or keeping money? With why you feel you don't have enough? Can the feelings in your body give any clues to what is going on in your subconscious? And can working with this not only help your physical and emotional health, but also your financial health?

This is a more advanced meditation technique, which will work with some of these ideas. It is broken down into five lessons- *master each lesson before moving onto the next.* This meditation technique is very powerful, and has nothing to do with the common notion that meditation is about "sitting around cross legged, not thinking about anything". It will engage the energies of your own body, chakras and aura for a powerful spiritual cleansing, thus clearing the way for personal growth and healing on all levels.

Lesson One – Grounding

Get comfortable sitting in a chair, feet on the floor, close your eyes, and relax. Now, bring your attention to you body, noticing how it feels; Is there any tightness, gripping, numbness, pain or agitation anywhere in your body?

Take a deep breath, and notice the base of your spine, which is your 1st chakra. The 1st chakra is where you will create a "grounding cord". When you make a grounded connection to the Earth, it stabilizes your body, and allows you to release pent up energy back to the planet.

Mentally, see and feel a bright spot of energy at your 1st chakra. Notice what happens to your body when you say hello to your 1st chakra, notice how it feels.

Next, notice the planet- send a hello deep down into the center of the Earth. Notice how your body feels to acknowledge the center of the planet.

Next, you will create a grounding cord - imagine a picture you'd like to use; it could be a beam of light, a waterfall, a tree, an umbilical cord, a rope. Feel the bright spot of energy at the base of your spine, and send another hello to the center of the planet. Now, step back mentally, and connect your 1st chakra with the center of the planet using your image. Send your grounding cord deep down into the center of the planet. Notice what happens to your body when you connect the two points - does your body release energy? Do you feel yourself coming back, deeper into yourself? Do you feel more solid? More relaxed?

Take a deep breath, and consciously decide to release energy - just let go of your day, your job, your responsibilities, at least for now, and allow yourself to connect with your body. Release any pent up energy, any pain, stiffness, tension or blockages from anywhere in your body down through your grounding cord. How does it feel to release energy? Notice your body, and use your grounding cord to release and relax. Notice if you're tight or tense anywhere- these are points where you may be carrying foreign energy- we can pick up energy from other people, from places and situations, and store it in our bodies. Say hello to them,

84

and let go- don't force or push the energy out, just let it drop out. Release all the foreign energy point by point, letting it fall through your body and down your grounding cord, back to the center of the Earth.

When all of the negative energies are released, and you feel very relaxed, you'll need to replenish your energy- but you don't want to replace it with the same energy you just released!. Instead, imagine a golden sun above your head, and call back your own energy from where ever you left it- at work, with other people, wherever. Make your sun big and bright, and let it flow through the top of your head and into all the places you've released. Let it flow through your entire body, filling up your feet, your hands, your fingers. If you want, make another sun.

When you're full, take a deep breath, open your eyes, stretch, and enjoy the feeling of being grounded.

Lesson Two - Creating Space

Get comfortable in your chair, take a deep breath, and say hello to your body. How do you feel? Settle in, close your eyes, and notice your entire body, especially your skin. Notice your size- how does it feel?

Notice your 1st chakra and the center of the planet, and send a hello to the two points. Create a grounding cord and connect. How does your body feel to connect and release energy?

Bring your awareness to your body again. Notice your "space"- your space is your aura. Become aware of this energy around you, feel its size, imagine a bubble of energy under your feet, over your head, behind you, in front of you. What happens to your body when you notice this space, your aura? How do you feel?

Continue to stay aware of your grounding cord. You can carry negative and foreign energy in your aura, too. Release any negative and foreign energy from your aura, (you don't need to identify it) just release it, and let it go.

Take a deep breathe. Now, notice your room - take your aura, and extend it to fill up the room. How does that feel? Sometimes your aura is big, sometimes it's small- do you feel you lose a sense of yourself, if you extend it too big? Now, extend it to encompass the building- how does that feel? Are you comfortable doing this? If it feels uncomfortable, try it anyway, just for the experience.

Now bring your aura back to the room, then back to your body, about two feet around your body. Next, pull it in another foot, then pull it in to six inches. How does that feel? Do you feel like you don't have enough space? Now bring it back to about two feet. Find a comfortable place. Sometimes just moving your aura around shakes out the alien and negative energy.

Notice your grounding cord, and continue to release energy. Now, get the idea of "owning" your space- in the owning and creating of space for yourself, you set the stage to heal yourself, as a spirit. Once you feel that ownership, create a golden sun, and bring your energy back from where you left it. Make the sun at least as big as your space, or even bigger. Bring the sun in, fill up your body and your aura. When you are ready, open your eyes, stretch, and enjoy the feeling of owning your space.

Lesson Three - The center of your head

Get comfortable, take a deep breath, notice your surroundings, notice your body, and relax. Notice the base of your spine and send a hello to the center of the planet. Connect the two with a line of energy, creating a grounding cord.

Once you are grounded, take a deep breath, and notice where your attention is. Is it on your body, your spouse, on your job, on your kids? As you get an idea of where your attention is, get the idea of bringing it back to yourself, back to your body.

86

As an experiment, become aware of your right hand. Put your attention in the palm of your hand. Notice what it feels like to have your attention in the palm of your hand. Next, notice your left foot, *be* in your left foot. Notice your nose -let yourself *be* at the tip of your nose. Then notice your eyes- move back until your attention is right behind your eyes- how does it feel to be in the center of your head? Notice what you find there- is it noisy? Are there thoughts there, or other people? Notice what is there, then notice that *you* are not any of these things, - *you* are the *awareness* in the center of your head.

Now, take a deep breathe, and release whatever it is you've found in the center of your head. Release it down your grounding cord, just let go of those thoughts, images and sensations. What happens when you let go? Notice how much room there is in the center of your head- as you let go, does that give *you* more room?

Now decide how you can create the center of your head as a sanctuary for yourself. You can create a beautiful room, or a landscape, a color, a feeling of warmth. Create it just for yourself. Is it big enough? Notice what happens to your body when you settle into the center of your head. Acknowledge your body, and yourself in the center of your head.

Next, create a golden sun, and let it flow through the center of your head. Make another sun, and let it flow through and fill up the rest of your body. When you are all full, open your eyes, stretch, and enjoy the new perspective from the center of your head.

Lesson Four – Separation

Relax, take a deep breath, and say hello to your 1st chakra. Send a hello into the center of the planet, and create a grounding cord.

Put your awareness into the center of your head. Imagine a big golden sun, and call back all your energy into that golden sun. Once you've collected up all your energy, allow the golden sun to flow through the top of your head, through the center of your head, and fill up your entire body. Do you feel a change once you're grounded and filled with your own energy?

Now, about eight inches from your forehead, get an image of your favorite flower, or maybe a bubble, or a miniature sun. Can you sense it? Can you feel it? Now release this image, and create another one- it could be another flower, or bubble or sun, or you could experiment with something different. Now release this image, just let it go, let it float away.

Notice the center of your head, notice the space around you, find the edge of your space, your aura. Notice you can also use your grounding cord to ground your aura.

Now, in front of you, get another image of a flower, or bubble or sun, but this time, with the idea that this image represents you, on an energy level. What does this image look like? Is it vibrant or dull? Solid or wilted? If you don't like it, release it and make another- just do this until you get something you like.

Now set your image on the edge of your aura. Allow it to be between you and all the energies around you. Allow it to provide some separation between the demands and expectations the world has of you. Get a sense of your job- let it be between you and your job. Get a sense of a person you work with- let your image be between you and this person, giving you space. You can even use it to give yourself space from your family.

As you find your separation from the things around you, you create more space for yourself. This space gives you the freedom to be you, to enjoy your own energy and ideas. Think of something you are supposed to be doing, a task, and allow yourself some space from it. How does that feel?

Allow your image to remain at the edge of your aura. Once you've found a sense of separation, create a golden sun, and fill yourself up. As you fill up, get a sense of owning your space, and owning your ability to be separate from the energies, expectations, people and things around you.

Lesson Five - Running Energy

Settle in, take a deep breath, and relax into your body. Notice the base of your spine, and send a hello to your 1st chakra. Notice the center of the planet, and send a hello to it. Then create a grounding cord, and connect these two points with a grounding cord.

Now bring your attention behind your eyes, into the center of your head. Notice your space, notice your body, notice your grounding.

Create your favorite separation image, and set it out in front of you, right at the edge of your aura. This allows you to separate from the energy around you, and go within.

Take a deep breath, and be aware of yourself in the center of your head. Then notice your feet. Right in the arch of each foot are your feet chakras. Say hello to your feet chakras, and allow them to open up.

Now, send a hello into the center of the planet, and look deep within the planet for some Earth energy. It might be a color, an image, a vast underground lake, or a great, glowing underground pool of lava.

Bring that Earth energy up, like a line of energy, coming up through the planet. Allow your feet chakras to draw this energy up, let it flow through your legs, and imagine the Earth energy flowing up through your legs to the 1st chakra. When the energy reaches the 1st chakra, allow it to fall back down your grounding cord. Notice what happens to your body when you run Earth energy.

Take a deep breath, notice yourself in the center of your head, and notice that the Earth energy keeps on flowing- once it starts, it automatically keeps flowing, like a siphon.

Next, notice the top of your head, your crown chakra. Say hello to your crown chakra, and imagine opening it up. Send a hello out to the Universe, go way out, past the atmosphere, past the planet, beyond the Solar System, way out into space. Now, find an energy you'd like to bring in. Start to call that energy down to the top of your head, right into the back part of your crown chakra. Allow that energy to flow down your back channels, on either side of your spine, into the 1st chakra.

Allow the Earth energy and the Cosmic energy to mix within the 1st chakra, and then let it flow back up through the front channels. As it flows through your body, it cleans out and energizes all your chakras.

When it reaches your 5th chakra at your throat, allow some energy to flow down your arms, and out through your fingers.

The rest of the energy will flow up through your crown chakra, and fountain out of your head, into your aura.

Take a deep breath, be aware of yourself in the center of your head, and notice what it feels like to run energy.

Allow the energy to flow as long as you like. When you are ready, create a golden sun of your own energy above your head. Call back all your energy, and collect it up into a bright, hot golden sun. Then let it flow through your head, filling up your entire body.

As you master the technique, try running different colors of Cosmic energy through your aura. You can use the colors related to the chakras, or any other color that comes to mind. See how running blue, green, yellow, pink, red, violet or blue makes your feel. If a particular color makes you feel good, go ahead and run it!

Lesson Six – Creating

Use all the meditation tools you have learned up til now, and get grounded, create some space, get into the center of your head, find some separation, and begin running your energy.

This next technique will be similar to the separation technique; in front of you, get an image of a flower, or bubble or sun, or whatever image you like to use, and explode it. Make another one, and explode that one too. Now make another one, and use that one for your creation.

Start to get an idea of what you want to create. Imagine it, feel it, and love it. Get a picture of it. Put that picture into your flower, bubble, or sun, and put as much detail into it as you can, think or and imagine every little detail you can. Just imagine it going right into your image. Now, see yourself in the creation; see yourself having it, put yourself right in there with it, having.

Next, ground this image, create a grounding cord to make it more solid. And as you ground it, if there is any energy in it that is not yours, any energy that says you can't have it, alters it, or makes it difficult to see it clearly, ground it out, just let it drain out of the picture, and let the whole creation get brighter.

Now, take this picture, and bring it into your aura. Notice how you feel, how your body feels, when experience this creation. Move it back out of your aura, and experience having it, and owning it. It is yours.

Next, call all of your *own energy* back from this image, bring it back to yourself. When this is done, release it into the Universe, just let it go, and float away to the center of the Cosmos.

Create another flower, bubble or sun in front of you, and gather up all the energy that might prevent you from having your creation, anything that says it is not possible, you are not good enough, etc, and release it into your image. When this is done, explode it, blow it up, to relase and neutralize that energy.

Create a golden sun over your head, and create lots of energy for you to have your creation into this sun. Bring that golden sun into the top of your head, filling your entire body and aura.

So that's it. Practice releasing the trapped, negative energy from your body, and running pure, clean energy from our Mother Earth and the Cosmos. Practice giving yourself "space", and refresh yourself with *your own* golden sun energy. You may be surprised with the cleansing effect these exercises have on your body, and you may also be surprised with what gets released! You may experience emotions, thoughts, remember events or people.... Let them go! Releasing the blockages will allow your energy to flow more freely, healing your body, mind, spirit, and hopefully your outer life circumstances, including your ability to get rich!

Daily Practice #1 What do you think about?

Your subconscious mind is not as mysterious or as inaccessible as you might think..... do you know that same old running dialog you keep going over and over in your head? What are you thinking about when you wake up in the morning? What are the things you keep telling yourself? What are the thoughts you are pushing away, and ignoring?

This project is to help you get in touch with what is really going on in your head.

You will need-

A small pocket size day book calendar

This is very simple- Every day, you will-
#1- keep track of what you are thinking about *that is **not** helpful towards your goals.* You will probably need to create a sort of short hand or

abbreviated notation of what you are thinking about- guaranteed, it will more than fill a page, so try and create a symbol for different types of thoughts, like a heart for relationships, dollar sign for money, etc. These are the thoughts that say, I'm not good enough, I don't have enough, blaming others for your problems, dwelling on and worrying about things you can't change, etc. You know what I am talking bout! Remember, you are to "fill your leisure hours, contemplating your vision". How can you do this, when you are filling your leisure hours (or minutes) contemplating your stupid, low paying job, your disadvantaged childhood, the aggravation your family causes you, etc, etc.

#2- Make "chicken scratches" for every negative thought you think during the day. ~~IIII~~

You will be AMAZED at how many little lines you mark down, one after another! But this will lessen, the more you listen to the self hypnosis program, and are mindful of your thoughts.

#3- This part ties in with the next Work Project. For every thought you give towards your goals, to contemplating your vision, give yourself $100.

Daily Practice #2- What is your time really worth?

For this next project, you will need either a notebook, or an accounting ledger. The accounting ledger would be more "official", but if you don't have one, a plain notebook will do.

OK, so how much money did you make last year? $20,000? $30,000? More? Less? Whatever you made, double it. This is going to be your new financial goal.

So, let's use $20,000. Double that equals $40,000. That would be your financial goal- to put down $40,000 on your tax return.

Next, take off the last three 0's off whatever your goal is- so if it is $40,000 you would have $40. This is what you will symbolically pay yourself for everything you do that leads towards your goal..... feels nice to make that per hour, doesn't it?

For every hour on your job, you will mark down your symbolic hourly wage.

For every hour you spend commuting, you will pay yourself this.

For every hour you spend working to build your own business, you will pay yourself this.

For all the research, phone calls, time driving, time on the computer, pay yourself.

Do you need to pay attention to your health? Pay yourself every time you exercise, choose the right foods, do whatever it is you need to do. What about education? Pay yourself for going to classes. Do you need to work on being patient? Polite? Persistent? Every time you do what you need to do, to advance yourself both financially, and as a person, reward yourself, with symbolic cash! Nothing motivates like money!

OK, so everyday you will keep track of everything you do that advances you towards both your financial goals, AND the goals that will improve you as a person. Write down each activity on a line in the ledger book, then add up all your time and the associated $$$. Remember from the last Work Project, you are also giving yourself $100 for every time you "contemplate your vision."

All your hard work will add up very quickly! When I first discovered this technique, I had more than $20,000 in my "account" within the first month!

Now, for the part you are *not* going to like- you will need to subtract every "real dollar" you earn from your symbolic dollars. So on pay day, subtract your check. When your business brings in money, subtract that (less costs, of course) As time goes on, you will be subtracting more and more (because you will be making more money!) But even so, you will be absolutely astounded at how much you will bring in by "doing every day, all that can be done".

Sure, this is "play money", but if you do this every night before you go to bed, it will be a very good exercise for you subconscious mind- imagine going to bed every night, with "money in the bank"! This exercise also serves the very important purpose of getting you used to the idea of *being worth more*. I used to work for non-profit group homes, and I got very used to the idea that I was only worth $10 an hour, since that's how much any job I could get from the newspaper paid. The year that I started this, I made $40,000, by working 60-100 hour weeks, every week! So when I started paying myself $80 an hour, I had $40,000 in my "symbolic account" in less than 2 months! It felt like, "Wow! So *is this* how much money all these 'rich people' around me make?" I could really see how it could add up fast to buy a nice car or even a house. *The point is, you need to get used to the idea that you and your time are worth more!*

My first goal was $80,000 (2 X $40,000) By the time I had approximately $320,000 in my symbolic account, *I had reached my real life goal of $80,000 a year.* So multiply your goal by 4, right now- how much is it? I estimate, that you will reach your real life goal by the time you have that amount in your symbolic account.

This won't happen overnight, but it can happen faster than you think! Spend your leisure hours, contemplating your vision, and do all that can be done, and you will be amply rewarded!

Daily Practice #3- Write It Out

So what do you want? The next work project requires-

A Blank Book or Scrap Book

This project is easy and fun- simply write out what you want. You will find that you may want to keep refining your vision as it develops. For instance, at first, you might just think, "I want to move to a better neighborhood, to a better house." OK, write that down. Eventually, you might get an idea for a specific neighborhood, and a more specific home. Keep refining your vision.

Same goes for a new job, a car, the type of business you want to have. Keep refining your vision!

The second part of this project is fun- since the mind and subconscious mind is impressed with pictures, you can cut out pictures of what you want- what is your ideal home? Look through magazines, and see what you want. What kind of car would you like? Cut out a picture! If you can draw, go for it! Put your vision down on paper!

The subconscious also responds to symbols- another fun and interesting idea is to create symbols for what you want- some aspects of your dream are not going to be found in a magazine to cut and paste, so you can also create your own symbols to draw your dream to you.

Also use this scrap book for writing down inspiring quotes, saving news stories that inspire you, to record your own successes! Use this book to visually record your dream, and the progress you are making towards it.

Daily Practice #4- Your Handwriting!

You may already know that a person's handwriting can reveal a lot about their character and personality…. What does yours reveal about you? The science of graphology is the study of handwriting, and the sub-science of "graphotherapy" claims that you can improve yourself through improving your handwriting. The theory is, that your handwriting is a sort of reflection of the neuropathways within your brain, *and that by changing your handwriting, you can change those neuropathways.* The subjects of graphology and graphotherapy require an entire book in itself, and I certainly can not analyze your personal handwriting here, but I can offer a few tips.

Try to keep your letters upright, not slanting far forward, and not slanting backward- it is best to keep your letters tall and upright. Also, does a line of your writing slant downward? Upward? Or straight across? Once again, it is best to keep things straightforward.

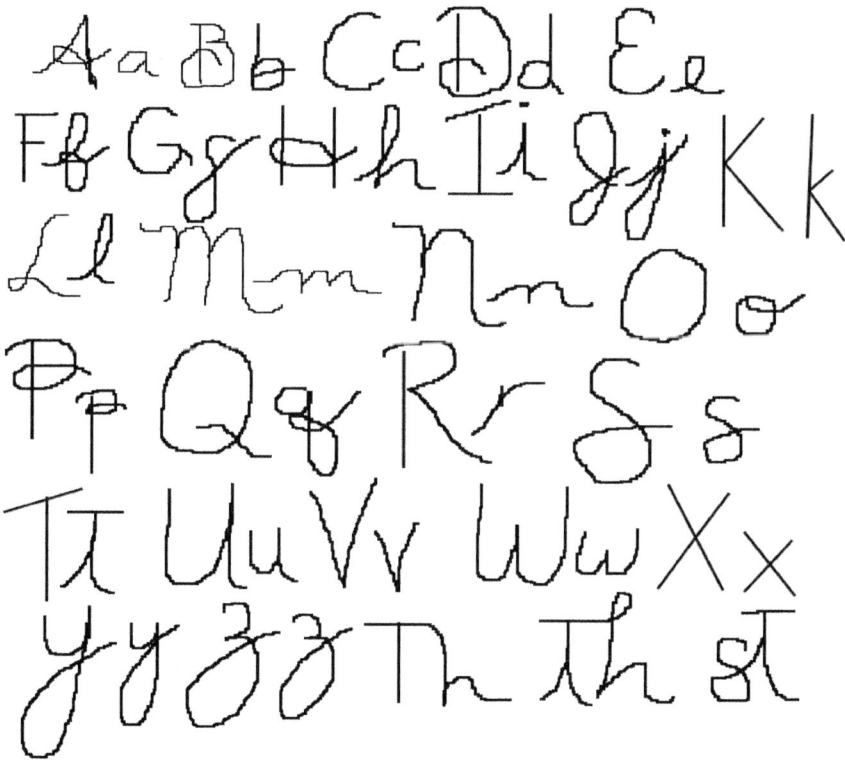

Above are letters drawn in the way that graphotherapists recommend for success- pay particular attention to your F's and T's. Skinny lower case F's can reflect a sort of "poverty consciousness", make them nice and fat!

Another common mistake in handwriting we have all learned is to cross our lower case T's in the middle; for greatest success, cross your lower case T's high, right at the top. Take care not to slant your cross bars down. If you will notice on the examples drawn above, the crossbars on the I and T are slightly slanted up- a higher sense of self esteem! Also pay attention to how you combine the small T with H and S.

Professional graphologists suggest practicing your handwriting for 20 minutes a day, for 40 straight days- if you miss a day, start all over! I know this Daily Practice seems a little off the wall, but if you are writing down what you want, and keep a daily tally of your "symbolic income" in a handwriting that reflects your current poverty consciousness, what might you manifest? More of the same? Graphotherapy can be used as just one more way to "reprogram" your mind towards greater prosperity and wealth! So, practice your handwriting with the above letters for 20 minutes a day, and incorporate it into your other daily practices and your daily life. You may be surprised to find you are literally "writing your own ticket" to success!

(For the MOST EFFECTIVE daily practice, you can purchase Dr. Jane Ma'ati Smith's "Science of Getting Rich" binaural beat self hypnosis and subliminal audio program from her website www.subliminalselfhypnosis.com or at Amazon.com to compliment this book)

Daily Practice #5- Using and Activating Reiki Symbols
The Japanese Symbol for Reiki

In Master level Reiki, you have access to the Sacred Reiki Symbols. These are handed down from Master to Master, and are used for attuning others into the Reiki Energy, and more importantly, they can be used for healing and protection. In this very special section, I will pass these symbols along to you; I have already charged them for you, with the intent of clearing the blockages to your wealth and prosperity.

The Reiki symbols are a means of focusing your attention, in order to connect with the particular healing frequencies symbolized by these signs. These healing frequencies have also been imbedded into the self hypnosis and subliminal audios which go with this program.

On the following pages are the five Reiki symbols I learned from my Master, which I now pass on to you!

CHU KU RAY

Pronounced "choh-koo-ray"

"The Power Symbol"

"God and Man Coming Together" or "I have the key"

The principal use of this symbol is to increase Reiki power. It draws Energy from around you, and it focuses it where you want to.

Make the sign over your heart, and say the words Cho Ku Rei 3 times, while imagining pictures of yourself with increased wealth.

It is an all-purpose symbol. It can be used for anything, anywhere, anytime, such as to cleanse negative energies, for spiritual protection, to bless food, water, medicine, herbs, *to aid in manifestation,* to seal energies after you do the other exercises in this book, and to empower other Reiki Symbols

Hint- If you wish to use the symbol to bring Energy to yourself, reverse it. Use it as drawn to help other people.

SEI HEI KI
Pronounced "say-hay-key"
The Mental/Emotional Symbol

"God and Man Coming Together" or "The Key to the Universe"

This symbol is used primary for mental and emotional healing, and for calming the mind. It is very useful for psychic protection and cleansing, to activate the Ki energy, to balance the right and left brain (a VERY complimentary symbol I have used with the binaural beat component of the audio programs!) This symbol also aids in removing addictions, healing past traumas clearing emotional blockages and removing negative energies and bad vibrations (including the mental addictions, past traumas, blockages and negative energies that keep you poor!)

This symbol restores emotional balance and harmony. Trace it over your abdomen while saying the words SEI HEI KI (pronounced "say-hay-key") slowly and deliberately three times. You can also trace this symbol and place it under your pillow while you sleep, to encourage peaceful sleep, and wonderful dreams of wealth and prosperity!

HON SHA ZE SHO NEN
Pronunciation: Hanh-shah-zay-show-nen
The Distance Symbol

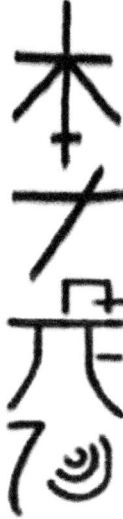

"The God in Me Greets the God in You, to Promote Enlightenment and Peace"

This is the distance healing symbol, and it is used to send Reiki over distance and time (past, present, and future), to anyone at anytime. I have this symbol posted in a secret, password protected file on the get-rich-mp3-download.com website, with prayers, specially attuned MP3 sound files and healing energy, constantly broadcasting out to all who use this program!

If you wish to use this to help another person, place your hand over it, close your eyes, and imagine sending healing energy and love to that person- yes, it's that easy to send out good vibrations to anyone and everyone!

TAM-A-RA-SHA

Pronunciation: Tam-ara-sha

The Balancing Factor

This symbol is a balancing and unblocking symbol. It grounds and balances energy, helping to unblock the chakra energy centers along the spine, allowing the energy to flow ore freely and abundantly.

To use this for prosperity, try drawing the symbol with your finger over each of your chakras, especially the root, navel, heart and brow chakras. Or, you can visualize this symbol during meditation. Begin at the root chakra, and visualize this symbol rising up, clearing all your chakras as it goes!

It is also a nice talisman to carry with you in your wallet- simply draw it on a slip of paper, and keep it with your money!

DAI KO MYO

Pronunced "dye-ko-me-o"

The Master Symbol

This is the most powerful symbol in Reiki. **It can be used only by Reiki Masters**. I have placed this symbol in a password protected, secret file on the get-rich-mp3-download.com website, along with prayers, specially attuned MP3 sound files and healing energy. I have charged it to work 24/7 on behalf of anyone who sincerely works this "Get Rich" program!

This symbol is used to heal the soul; since it deals with the soul and our spiritual self, it heals disease, illness (and conditions such as poverty) *from the original source,* in the aura and energy field.

It helps to foster enlightenment and peace. It also works to clear blockages to becoming more intuitive- the better your intuition, the clearer your vision will be to finding your way to the peace, happiness and prosperity you seek! Like the Lightening it symbolizes, this symbol brings profound life changes on an energetic level.

METHODS FOR REIKI SYMBOL ACTIVATION

The symbols can be activated in any of the following ways:

By drawing them with your palm, while projecting energy outwards

By drawing them with your finger

By visualizing them

By spelling the symbol's name three times.

By saying the symbol's name three times.

*You can use whatever method you wish, but don't forget that it's the **intent** that counts.*

To help your friends and family with Reiki symbols-

First place the symbol in the palm of your own hand, and then redraw or visualize the same symbol on the other person's crown chakra, the palm of that person's hand, or if they are sick or in pain, the areas to be treated (of course, please recognize, that doing this does not replace proper medical treatment for serious illness!)

With practice, the actual symbols will become less relevant, and your focus will change to the *intent* of the specific symbols.

Daily Practice #6- The Sweet Smell of Success!

Take out the crispest, cleanest, newest bill in your wallet right now..... and smell it! That's right, *I want you to memorize the sweet smell of money!* Our memories operate in all our senses, and the sense of smell is a powerful one. Every time you pay for something, smell a bill, and think to yourself "Unlimited Wealth", and pass it along to the next person.

BREATHING

Most of us haven't learned to breathe; shallow breathing can cause problems on many levels. When we are constantly 'holding our breathe', carbon dioxide will build up in the blood stream, causing unnecessary anxiety, and clouded thinking.

Breathing deeply and slowly, is the optimum way to breathe; relax your diaphragm, and draw your breathe all the way down into your belly. Pause, then fully exhale, feeling your warm breathe as it passes through the center of your body, up into your 'Third Eye', and out your nose.

Breathing into your chakras is a technique worth learning and using. Breathing all the way down to the navel chakra in your belly, and breathing out through your crown chakra at the top of your head will produce a sense of euphoria during meditation, though it may be too disorienting to do while out in the 'real world'. Breathing into your heart chakra, and exhaling through your brow chakra is a good basic technique to use in your everyday dealings with the 'real world', and, it can facilitate your ability to "manifest from the heart". Whenever you think of it (all the time is best) breathe into your heart, fully expanding the energy there, and breathe in "unlimited wealth". (At first you can think the words, but eventually, it should become a *feeling.)* Fully exhale all the fear, doubt, and limitations that are holding you back. Inhale unlimited wealth, exhale doubt, fear and limitation!

Some of these ideas and techniques concerning energy, meditation, chakras, and such may seem foreign to the way you have been taught to *think*. But that's the point- most of us have been encouraged to think, but not to *experience* ourselves, others, or our world as an energy, or even as a physical body. Our ability for critical thought is what separates us from the rest of the animal kingdom, for good and for worse. The psychic 'sixth sense' may be nothing more than the human animal's natural instincts, and an animal's instincts guide it to the environments that will allow it to flourish. Our 'critical' thinking can often be the biggest stumbling block; how much of what you think you want is really the influence of what society, your family, or your job expects of you? This energetic 'static' will interfere with following your instincts, and your instincts are your natural 'tool' for finding that which will allow *you* to truly flourish!

Put It Into Practice! Real World Resources!

Believing in yourself and the Universe, changing your mind set, and practicing self hypnosis can go a long way, but if you *really* want to make *money*, you will have to do *something* in the *real world*. Remember, Wallace Wattles tells us, that the Universe provides wealth and opportunity through the everyday channels of commerce and trade mankind has created. For a plentitude of ideas for making money on the web, go to this webpage- get-rich-mp3-download.com/resources.html It is my gift to you, to help you get started on your own!

Many "manifestation experts" will tell you to "focus only on the end result, the final goal". Well, I am here to tell you otherwise! Your final goal may be to live on a tropical island, but realistically, how is that going to happen (winning the lottery excluded!) You are more than likely going to have to do *something* to earn your wealth. ***And once you decide on*** *what you are going to do, break it down into smaller steps, and start your visualizing and creating from there! You need to keep the final result in mind always, but just focus your attention on one thing at a time, and that thing is what you need to do next!*

In this way, you will reach your goal one step at a time, and not intimidate yourself with something that might seem unattainable from where you are now. Remember, figure out what you want to do, then break it down into steps (and even sub-steps) and start up your ladder there!

(You can purchase Dr. Jane Ma'ati Smith's "Science of Getting Rich" binaural beat self hypnosis and subliminal audio program from her website www.subliminalselfhypnosis.com or at Amazon.com to compliment this book)

To your Health Wealth and Happiness!

Dr. Jane Ma'ati Smith C. Hyp. Msc. D.

For "The Science of Getting Rich" self hypnosis and subliminal CD or download, plus many more self help books and CDs by Dr. Jane Ma'ati Smith C.Hyp. Msc.D., plus downloadable books and MP3s, visit www.subliminalselfhypnosis.com

"The Universe desires you to have everything you want to have. Nature is friendly to you plans. Everything is naturally for you."

☺

"Make up your mind this is true. You need not hesitate about asking largely."

~Wallace Wattles

Printed in Great Britain
by Amazon

46620417R00067